I0439168

OS Study
MMS 2004-047

Supply Network for Deepwater Oil and Gas Development in the Gulf of Mexico: An Empirical Analysis of Demand for Port Services

Final Report

MMS **U.S. Department of the Interior**
Minerals Management Service
Gulf of Mexico OCS Region

OCS Study
MMS 2004-047

Supply Network for Deepwater Oil and Gas Development in the Gulf of Mexico: An Empirical Analysis of Demand for Port Services

Final Report

Authors

Jay Jayawardana
Anatoly Hochstein

Prepared under MMS Contract
1435-01-01-CA-31154
by
UNO National Ports and Waterways Institute
University of New Orleans
College of Urban & Public Affairs
New Orleans, Louisiana 70148

Published by

U.S. Department of the Interior
Minerals Management Service
Gulf of Mexico OCS Region

New Orleans
June 2004

DISCLAIMER

This report was prepared under a contract between the Minerals Management Service (MMS) and UNO National Ports and Waterways Institute. This report has been technically reviewed by MMS, and has been approved for publication. Approval does not signify that the contents necessarily reflect the views and policies of MMS, nor does mention of trade names or commercial products constitute endorsement or recommendation for use. It is, however, exempt from review and compliance with the MMS editorial standards.

REPORT AVAILABILITY

Extra copies of this report may be obtained from the Public Information Office (Mail Stop 5034) at the following address:

U.S. Department of the Interior
Minerals Management Service
Gulf of Mexico OCS Region
Public Information Office (MS 5034)
1201 Elmwood Park Boulevard
New Orleans, Louisiana 70123-2394

Telephone: (504) 736-2519 or
1-800-200-GULF

CITATION

Suggested citation:

Jayawardana, J. and A. Hochstein. 2004. Supply Network for Deepwater Oil and Gas Development in the Gulf of Mexico: An Empirical Analysis of Demand for Port Services; Final Report. Prepared by UNO National Ports and Waterways Institute. U.S. Dept. of the Interior, Minerals Management Service, Gulf of Mexico OCS Region, New Orleans, LA. OCS Study MMS 2004-047. 98 pp.

ABSTRACT

This report presents an empirical analysis of the demand for port services generated by the deepwater oil and gas industry during its phenomenal growth during the last decade. During this period, the deepwater oil production registered a nine-fold increase while the gas production increased sixteen fold. In addition, technological developments in seismic data acquisition, large deepwater field discoveries, and the innovative production systems have completely transformed the industry and the logistical support network. Although the logistical support system is a vital component of the industry, empirical studies analyzing the supply network adjustments from the perspective of port services are currently not available. Therefore, the demand analysis in this report will fill that void and is expected to be useful for port planning and investment decisions.

The methodological approach followed in the analysis was determined by the nature of port activities at each port and data availability. For example, for Port Fourchon the demand for port services was estimated using time-series data from 1992 to 2001. The variable relationships between several industry variables and port services such as port tonnage, truck traffic and inland barge traffic were estimated using regression analysis. Similarly, for the Port of Morgan City specializing in shipbuilding, the demand relationships for vessel traffic on the Atchafalaya River and the industry variables were estimated.

The regression models for Port Fourchon indicated that for every additional OCS well drilled the truck traffic at the port will increase by about 673 trips a year, inland barge traffic by 7 trips, and the tonnage handled at the port by 11,400 tons. Similarly, another model predicted that for every mile of pipeline approved, truck traffic will increase by 217 trips, barge traffic by 3 trips, and port tonnage by 46,000 tons.

Using the above empirical estimates, demand forecasts were developed through 2010 for each variable. According to these estimates, truck traffic is expected to grow by 67 percent between 2001 and 2010, barge traffic by 25 percent and the port tonnage by 100 percent.

The regression models estimated for the Port of Morgan City indicated that for every additional OCS well rigged the number of non-self propelled vessels on the Atchafalaya will increase by about 12 trips. The traffic forecasts through 2010 indicated a 62 percent growth for the period 2001 to 2010.

With more than 60 percent of the port tenants engaged in OCS related services, the Port of Iberia experienced continuous growth in the 1990's. Since activities at the Port of Iberia are concentrated on the assembly of prefabricated structures, repair and maintenance, a quantitative database with relevant demand and supply was not available. However, analytical models developed on port financial performance and infrastructure expansion indicated increasing demand for offshore services. The OCS service activities at the Port of Galveston have emerged as an important sector with an increasing share of waterfront land devoted to offshore activities and the location of several large-scale tenant operations in recent years.

A qualitative analysis of different port variables also indicate the extent of adjustments made by the ports during the period. For example during the 1992-2001 period, port tonnage handled increased seven-fold and port operating revenues increased by 82 percent at Port Fourchon. The operating revenues at the Port of Iberia increased three-fold during 1992-2000 the period. The amount of waterfront land allotted to OCS activities at the Port of Galveston increased twenty-fold during the same period.

Based on all the information in this report, it is evident that the ports have expanded infrastructure investment to meet the growing needs of the deepwater oil and gas industry. As the industry grew at a faster pace than the supply of port services during the period, the ports have enjoyed higher returns resulting in better financial performance. However, as the deepwater oil and gas industry reaches a plateau, more information is needed in port investment and planning decisions. This report is an attempt to provide such information.

TABLE OF CONTENTS

LIST OF FIGURES

LIST OF TABLES

ABBREVIATIONS, ACRONYMS, AND SYMBOLS

AADT	Average Daily Traffic
ac	acre
BNSF	Burlington Northern and Santa Fe Railroads
Chouest	Edison Chouest Offshore (ECO)/C Port Galveston, LP
CPA	Central Planning Area
COE	U.S. Army Corps of Engineers
DOCD	Development Operations Coordination Document
EPA	Eastern Planning Area
EP	Exploration Plans
ft	feet
ft^2	square feet
GIWW	Gulf Intracoastal Waterway
GOM	Gulf of Mexico
GVSR	Galveston Railroad, L.C.
LOOP	Louisiana Offshore Oil Port
LOS	Level of Service
mi	miles
MMS	U.S. Minerals Management Service
OCS	Outer Continental Shelf
PCDP	Louisiana Port Construction and Development Priority Program
POI	Port of Iberia
R-square (R^2)	Coefficient of Determination
RO/RO	Roll-on/Roll-off Vessels
UNO	University of New Orleans
UP	Union
V/C	Vehicle/Capacity Ratio
WPA	Western Planning Area

1. Executive Summary

1.1. Ports and the OCS Supply Network

An effective logistical support system is an important prerequisite for deepwater oil and gas exploration and development. In this intermodal transportation system, ports have emerged as pivotal activity centers connecting the onshore network with the waterborne offshore segment. In addition to cargo handling, ports also serve as industrial sites for large shipyards, equipment fabrication and repair, and value-added processing activities for both inputs and outputs of the industry.

1.1.1. Study Approach and Outline

The major objectives of this study are to define and analyze the nature of port services supporting the deepwater oil and gas exploration, and to estimate demand and supply adjustments made by both sectors in the 1990's. For this purpose, a database on port activities was developed for four major Outer Continental Shelf (OCS) ports in the Gulf of Mexico (GOM): Port Fourchon, Port of Morgan City, and Port of Iberia, Louisiana, and Port of Galveston, Texas. Using empirical data, quantitative estimates of supply and demand were developed for several port activity variables. Based on the parameter estimates derived from econometric models, growth forecasts were made through 2010.

The report is divided into five sections with an introduction in Chapter 2 and Chapters 3-6 devoted to analyzing the activities at each of the four ports: Port Fourchon (Chapter 3), Port of Morgan City (Chapter 4), Port of Iberia (Chapter 5), and Port of Galveston (Chapter 6).

1.1.2. Major Components of the System

The OCS supply network consists of three major components: the inland transportation network, the offshore sector, and the port sector (Figure 1.1). The port sector consists of public port authorities and private sector service providers jointly operating to deliver the supply needs of the industry.

1.2. Port Fourchon

Port Fourchon has developed into the largest GOM supply base for offshore oil and gas services due to its central location with easy access to the GOM and the availability of port infrastructure.. Distinct advantages to the port are its proximity to offshore installations in the Central Planning Area (CPA) and Eastern Planning Area (EPA) and its 300-foot (ft) wide navigational channel with a 24 ft depth. Since 44 percent of pending exploration plans (EP) have indicated Port Fourchon as their supply base, the market share of the port is expected to expand with industry growth[1].

1.2.1. Demand for Port Services

A database consisting of both port and OCS activity variables was developed to estimate the demand for port services generated by the offshore industry. Using data for the period 1992 to 2001, several regression models were specified to represent the demand for port services (Figure 1.2). Different variables trends were examined (Figure 1.3) prior to proceeding with the empirical analysis.

---

[1] *Deepwater Gulf of Mexico 2002: America's Expanding Frontier.* (U.S. Minerals Management Service, 2002)

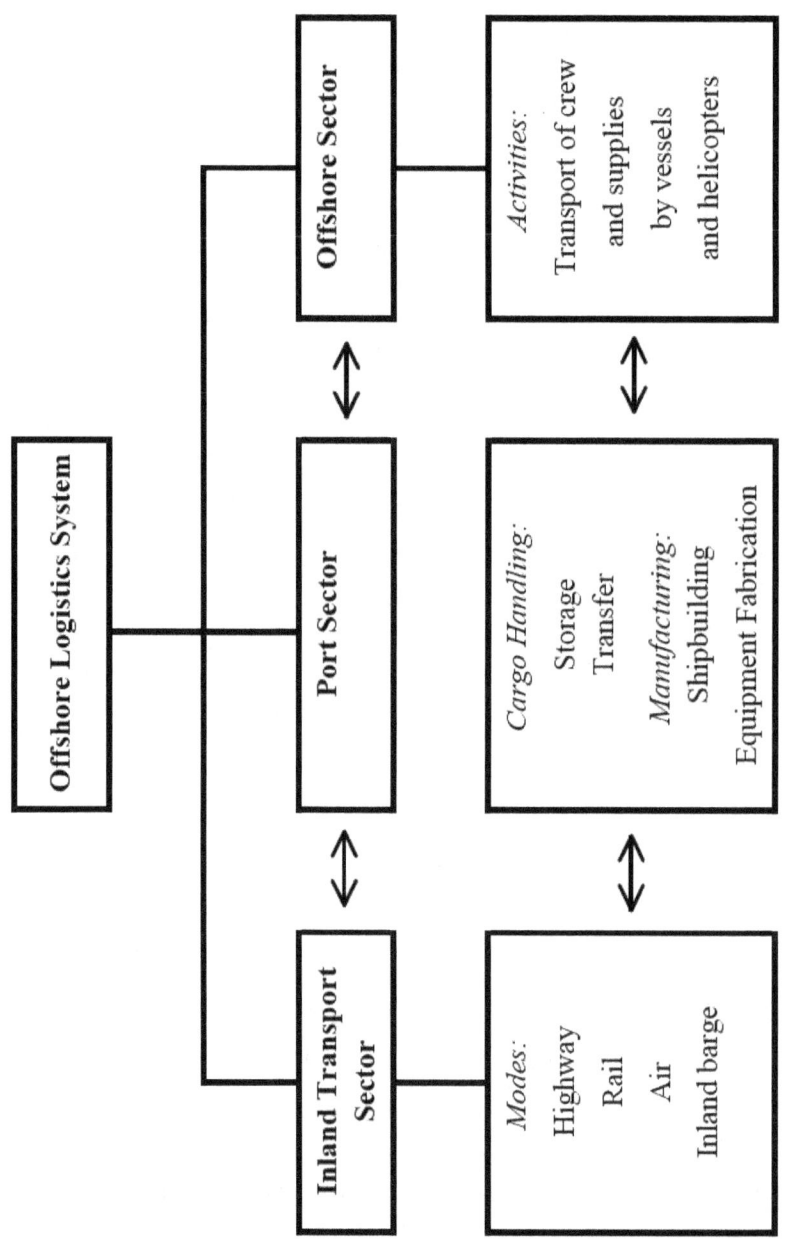

Figure 1.1. OCS Supply Network – Major Components.

Independent Variables
1. Total Number of OCS Wells Drilled
2. Number of OCS Exploratory Wells Drilled
3. Number of Pipeline Miles Approved

Dependent Variables
1. Number of Trucks South Bound on LA HWY 1
2. Number of Galliano Bridge Openings
3. Total Tons at Port

Regression Models		
Model Number	**Independent Variable**	**Dependent Variable**
1.1	Total OCS Wells Drilled	Trucks South Bound on LA HWY 1
1.2	Exploratory Wells Drilled	Trucks South Bound on LA HWY 1
1.3	Pipeline Miles Approved	Trucks South Bound on LA HWY 1
2.1	Total OCS Wells Drilled	Galliano Bridge Openings
2.2	Exploratory Wells Drilled	Galliano Bridge Openings
2.3	Pipeline Miles Approved	Galliano Bridge Openings
3.1	Total OCS Wells Drilled	Total Port Tonnage
3.2	Exploratory Wells Drilled	Total Port Tonnage
3.3	Pipeline Miles Approved	Total Port Tonnage

Figure 1.2. Model Specifications and Variable Relationships Estimated, Port Fourchon.

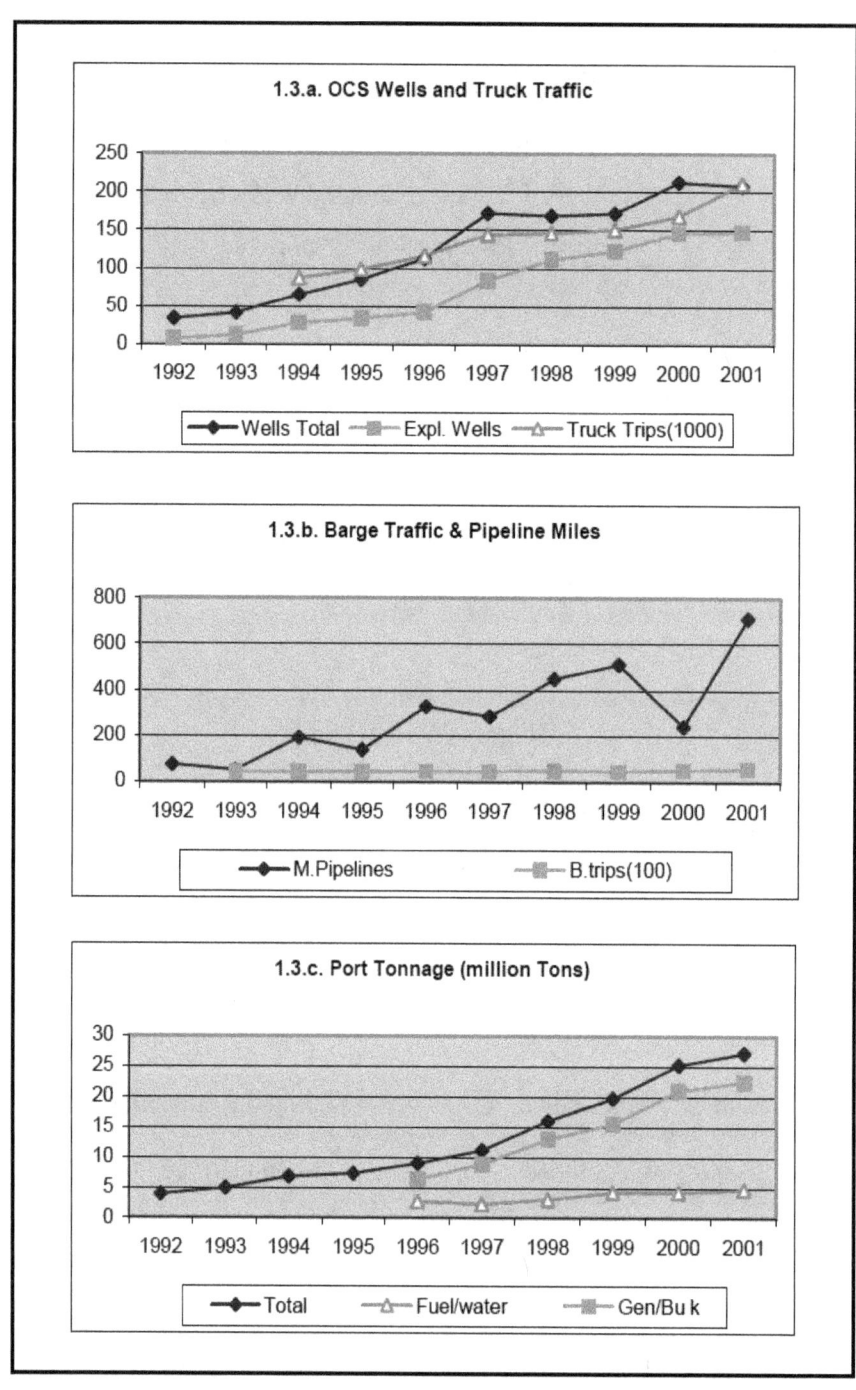

Figure 1.3. Variable Trends, Port Fourchon.

1.2.2. Empirical Analysis and Forecasts

Using regression analysis, the demand relationships for truck traffic, barge traffic, and cargo tonnage at Port Fourchon were estimated. While the estimates derived from all nine models were statistically significant and consistent, the three models with the highest R-square (R^2) in each category are shown in Table 1.1.

Table1.1

Regression Estimates for Truck Traffic, Inland Barge, and Cargo Tonnage, Port Fourchon

Independent Variable	Model No.	Intercept	Regression Coefficient	R^2	F-Value
Truck traffic on LA HWY 1					
Total OCS Wells	1:1	39,817 (2.39)*	672.8 (6.40)*	0.8723	40.98*
Inland barge traffic at Galliano Bridge					
OCS Exploratory Wells	2:2	4,142 (25.75*)	7.78 (4.61*)	0.7525	21.28*
Port cargo tonnage					
OCS Exploratory Wells	3:2	2.18 (1.95**)	0.1485 (11.98*)	0.9472	143.53*

Statistical significance levels at 5% and 10% are denoted by * and ** respectively.

Truck Traffic South Bound on LA Hwy 1

During the 1994-2001 period, truck traffic volume on Louisiana Highway 1 (LA Hwy 1 or LA HWY 1) at Port Fourchon increased from approximately 87,000 trips per (/) year (yr) to over 211,000 trips/yr indicating an annual growth rate of 13.5 percent. According to the empirical analysis, the demand relationship between truck traffic and all categories of OCS wells drilled is positive, and is estimated to increase by 673 trips for every additional well drilled (Regression Model 1:1, Table 1.1). Estimated truck traffic is projected to grow at an annual rate of 6 percent through 2010. At this rate, truck traffic volume in 2010 is estimated at 353,333 trips, an increase in 2001 traffic by 67 percent. Although the current pace of 13.5 percent growth associated with the initial phase of development tapers off over time a sustained annual rate of 6 percent will lead to capacity problems unless the necessary expansions are planned ahead of time.

Barge Traffic at Galliano Bridge

Inland barge traffic grew at a more modest rate of 4 percent a year during the period 1993-2001. Of the three models specified to estimate barge traffic, Regression Model 2.3, with the number of pipeline miles approved as the independent variable, provided statistically significant parameter estimates. Because of the time lag between the approval and implementation of pipeline projects, a two year lag variable was used in the model. For every mile of pipeline added, barge traffic is estimated to increase by three additional trips. Therefore, barge traffic is forecasted to increase from 5,717 trips/yr in 2001 to 7,129 trips/yr in 2010, an overall increase of 25 percent for the period with an annual growth of 2-3 percent.

Port Tonnage

Cargo tonnage at the port grew from 3.9 million tons/yr to 27.2 million tons/yr between 1992 and 2001, an increase of 24 percent a year. Regression Model 3:2 with the number of OCS exploratory wells drilled as the independent variable provided the 'best-fit' model for cargo tonnage with an R^2 value of 0.95. The model estimates that for every exploratory well drilled, 148,500 tons of cargo is generated at the port. The 2010 port tonnage estimate is 50.8 million tons. This equates to an annual growth rate of 7-8 percent with an overall doubling of the current tonnage volumes.

1.3. Port of Morgan City

Morgan City is an important onshore supply base currently serving several deepwater oil and gas installations. Morgan City's supply services are distinct from Port Fourchon's in several ways:

- Shipbuilding and repair activities at Morgan City are much more significant to the OCS logistics system,
- The public port plays a low-key role; OCS activities are mostly private sector operations, and
- The location of Morgan City, at the intersection of several major waterways, is an advantage.

1.3.1. Profiles of Major Operators

Table 1.2 shows the number of employees and the sales volumes of major firms engaged in offshore services at Morgan City. The magnitude of these numbers illustrates the significance of offshore operations at the port.

Table 1.2

Major Offshore Oil and Gas Service Firms, Morgan City

Name of Firm	Number Employed	Annual Sales ($millions)	Activity
Bollinger Marine Fabricators	400	25-100	Shipbuilding & repair
Cameron Corporation	268	10-25	Oil & gas field machinery
Conrad Industries, Inc.	200	15	Boat building & repair
Mc Dermott, Inc.	2,000	100-500	Oil & gas Field machinery
Superior Fabricators, Inc.	110	14	Structural metal fabricated
Swiftships Shipbuilders, LLC	245	40	Boat building & repair
Twin Bros. Marine Corp.	240	N/A	Shipbuilding & repair

1.3.2. Demand for Port Services

Several factors make it difficult to analyze the demand for port services at Morgan City. First, a database of port activities, like at Port Fourchon, is not available. Because of the proprietary nature of private sector operations at Morgan City, it is difficult to develop an adequate database for analysis. Second, the market share of port services at Morgan City is relatively low; therefore, models may not adequately reflect industry-wide changes at a macro level. Third, since the shipbuilding and repair services cater to a diversified set of domestic and foreign clients, it is more difficult to delineate the effects of the OCS oil and gas industry.

1.3.3. Empirical Analysis and Forecasts

Morgan City's main access channel is the Atchafalaya River which provides the vital link for the delivery of offshore supply services to the GOM. Therefore, vessel traffic is hypothesized to represent the level of port services for Morgan City. The number of non self-propelled vessel trips is used as the dependent variable in the regression models estimating the demand for port services. The oil and gas industry variables are similar to those defined for Port Fourchon. The trends of the industry variables and the port activity variables are shown in Figure 1.4.

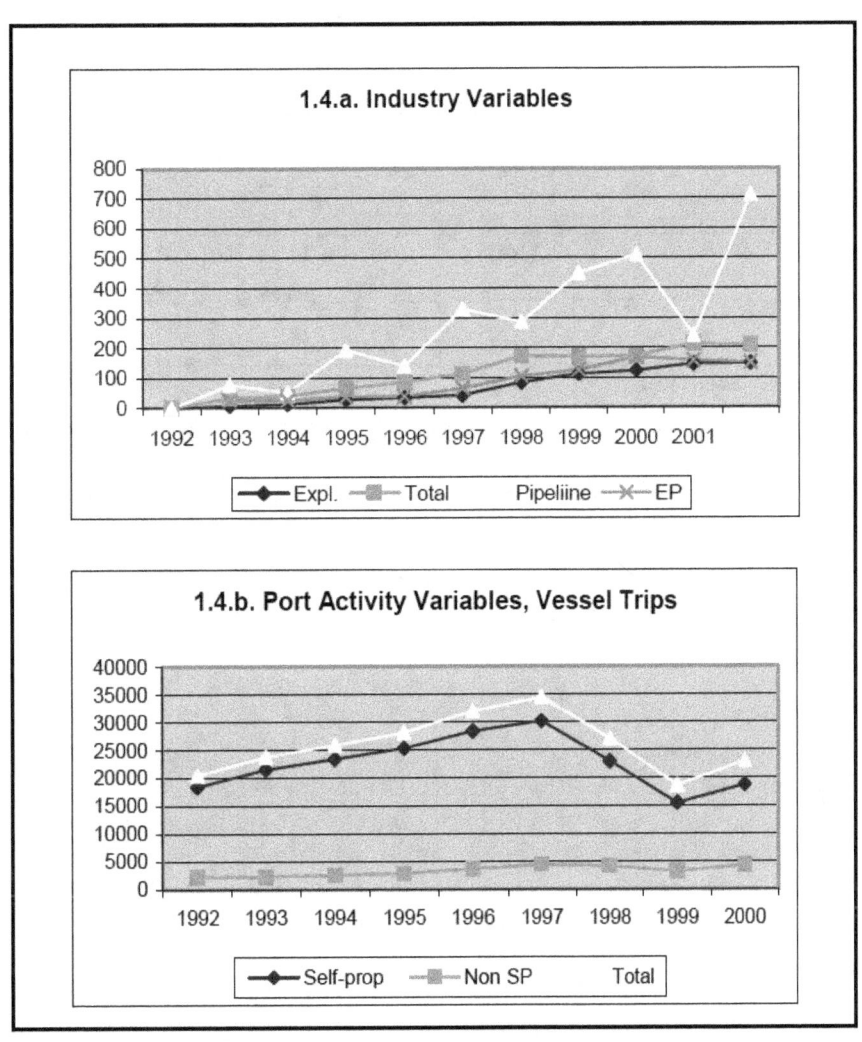

Figure 1.4. Variables Trends, Morgan City.

Variable Relationships between the Number of OCS Wells Drilled and Vessel Traffic

Four regression models were specified for the Port of Morgan City. The three models using different categories of OCS wells (development, exploratory, and total) as the explanatory variable provided statistically significant parameter estimates and high F-values (Table 1.3.). The models with the independent variables number of OCS development wells drilled (Regression Model 4.1) and total number of OCS wells drilled (Regression Model 4.3) explain more than 80 percent of the variations in non self-propelled vessel traffic trips. Surprisingly, the variable number of OCS development wells drilled, which provided the "best fit" model for Morgan City, was dropped as a variable in the Port Fourchon analysis. The results indicated that for every development well and exploratory well drilled on the OCS, the number of non self-propelled vessel trips to Morgan City increase by 40 and 13, respectively. The corresponding number of vessel trips for the total number of wells is 12.

Table 1.3

Regression Estimates for Vessel Traffic and Technical Relationships
Between Different Variables, Morgan City

Independent Variable[1]	Model No.	Intercept	Regression Coefficient	R^2	F-Value
Number of development wells-drilled	4.1	1129.5 (3.02)*	39.9 (6.0)*	0.8371	35.97
Number of exploratory wells drilled	4.2	2364.0 (7.28)*	13.40 (3.36)*	0.6181	11.33
Total number of wells drilled	4.3	1796.0 (6.21)*	12.21 (5.64)*	0.8195	31.77
Miles of pipeline approved (lagged by one year)	4.4	2544.4 (5.72)*	3.29 (2.21)**	0.4501	4.91

1/ The dependent variable for all regressions is number of non self-propelled vessel trips.
Statistical significance levels at 5% and 10% are denoted by * and ** respectively. Numbers in parentheses are t-values.

Port Activity Forecasts

The vessel trip forecasts were developed through 2010 following procedures similar to those described in Chapter 3 for Port Fourchon. The forecasts from regression models were compared with the forecasts of vessel trips derived from linear trend extrapolation. The projections derived from models were lower than the trend. For example, while the trend indicated 6,900 vessel trips in 2010 with an annual growth rate of 5 percent, the median forecast derived from using exploratory variables in the model was approximately 4.5 percent.

1.4. Port of Iberia

The Port of Iberia is located along the Commercial Canal approximately 7.5 miles (mi) north of the Gulf Intracoastal Waterway (GIWW), 9 mi north of Weeks Bay on the GOM, and 4.5 mi southwest of the city of New Iberia. The location and configuration of the Port of Iberia are strongly influenced by OCS supply activities; the port specializes in platform fabrication, repair, and maintenance.

1.4.1. Demand for Port Services

A large number of small-scale operators provide a variety of OCS services based at the public port. Because of the variety of operations, an appropriate time-series database including the major developments is not available for analysis. However, the demand generated by OCS activities and its effects on the Port of Iberia are clearly evident from a qualitative analysis of the following developments at the port:

- number of OCS service providers,
- infrastructure expansion and investment,
- demand for facilities,
- activities of tenants, and
- financial performance.

Number of OCS Service Providers at the Port

A survey conducted in 1999 indicates that 70.6 percent of the businesses in the Port of Iberia area are in some form connected to the offshore supply industry (Table 1.4).

Table 1.4

Classification of Businesses (1999), Port of Iberia

Industry	Number of Business Units	Percent of the Sample
The offshore supply industries:		
Fabrication	20	19.6
Repair Services	9	8.8
Other offshore services	43	42.2
Total offshore	72	70.6
Other Industries	30	29.4
Grand Total	102	100

Port Infrastructure Investment

In the 1990's, the Port of Iberia followed a systematic program to upgrade its facilities due to the demand pressures for port services. These upgrades include:

1. *Projects to provide basic port infrastructure and amenities (early 1990's)* - the development of a wastewater collection system, sanitary sewer collection, potable water system, etc.,
2. *Port expansion projects (mid 1990's)* - the development of a slip in a 170-acre (ac) lot was undertaken in 1995, and

9

3. *Port improvement projects with public and private sector cost sharing (late 1990's)* - improvements at the terminal such as building bulkheads, warehouses, etc. and sharing the costs with tenants.

Figure 1.5 shows capital expenditures at the port under the Louisiana Port Priority Program during the 1990-2000 period.

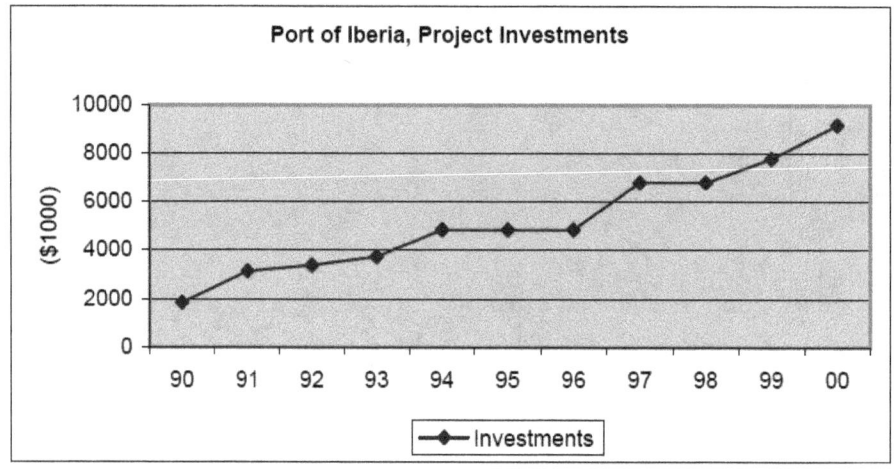

Figure 1.5. Capital Expenditures, Cumulative Trend (1990-2000), Port of Iberia.

Demand for Port Facilities

An analysis of the port's lease information indicates that 279 ac of waterfront property is leased to 47 tenants (Table 1.5). With 55 percent of the land leased beyond 2005, the port is assured of a stable revenue stream for the next 10-15 years.

Table 1.5

Analysis of Lease Operations, Port of Iberia

Lease Period	No. of Leases	Waterfront Acreage	Average Size (Acres)	Percent of Total Leased Acreage
2000-2005	31	123.6	4.0	44.3
2006-2010	12	96.7	8.1	34.7
2011-2020	4	58.6	14.7	21.0
Total	47	278.9	5.9	100

Source: Port of Iberia, Master Development Plan, 2000.

Financial Performance of the Port

Key financial indicators for the 1992 to 2000 period indicate favorable growth. While the port's operating revenues increased 205 percent, operating expenses increased by only 35 percent leading to a 170 percent increase in net income. Total assets of the port grew by more than 125 percent during this period.

1.5. Port of Galveston

The Port of Galveston is located on Galveston Bay 9.3 mi inland from the GOM. Galveston public port facilities are strategically located providing easy access to the GOM and the inland waterways network through GIWW. The Galveston Ship Channel serves as the main access channel to the port. It is maintained at a 40 ft depth and 1,200 ft width. Estimated sailing time from open sea to the public docks, located 9.3 mi on the Ship Channel, is approximately 30 minutes. In addition, the large industrial and commercial hub around the Houston Ship Channel to the west, serves as a great asset in providing specialized technical services.

1.5.1. Offshore Service Activities and Major Operators

Four major offshore service providers operate from the Port of Galveston:

1. Edison Chouest Offshore (ECO)/C Port Galveston, LP, at Edison Chouest Offshore Service Center
2. Pier 34 Manufacturing Facility operated by Cooper-Cameron Corp-Deep Flex Division,
3. Marine Repair Facility at Pier 14, operated by Smith-Hamm, Inc. and
4. Pelican Island Marine Repair Facility operated by First Wave/Newpark Shipbuilding-Pelican Island, Inc.

In April 2000, the Port of Galveston entered into a lease agreement with Edison Chouest for the development of an offshore multi-service terminal. The 100-ac site, located on Pelican Island, is an indication of the increase in demand for offshore services in the Western Planning Area (WPA). Edison Chouest plans to develop a multi-service facility known as C Port Galveston.

The port signed a five-year lease agreement with Cooper-Cameron Corporation in March 1999 for Pier 34. The pier's main facility is a terminal with a water depth of 40 ft and 44,500 square ft (ft^2) of covered space. The firm specializes in the manufacture of flexible pipes for the offshore oil and gas industry.

Marine Repair Facility at Pier 14, operated by Smith-Hamm, Inc., is engaged in the repair and maintenance of vessels and offshore rigs. Major infrastructure at the pier includes a 1,500-ft dock with a minimum water depth of 24 ft, and a staging area of 35,000 ft^2. In 1999, the company expanded its operations by leasing six additional acres.

First Wave/Newpark Shipbuilding-Pelican Island, Inc. operates Pelican Island Marine Repair Facility, a 110-ac vessel repair and maintenance facility. The company operates a network of five yards offering repair and maintenance services, new construction, and environmental services.

1.5.2. Growth Trends in OCS Services

Port-owned waterfront land increased from about 299 ac in 1965 to approximately 850 ac in 2000, almost tripling the size of the port. The recent additions of land have been leased mostly by offshore service providers. As a result of the above developments, port tenants serving the offshore industry have increased their share of port-owned land by 23 percent (27% in 2000 v. 4% in 1993) over the last seven years (Figure 1.6).

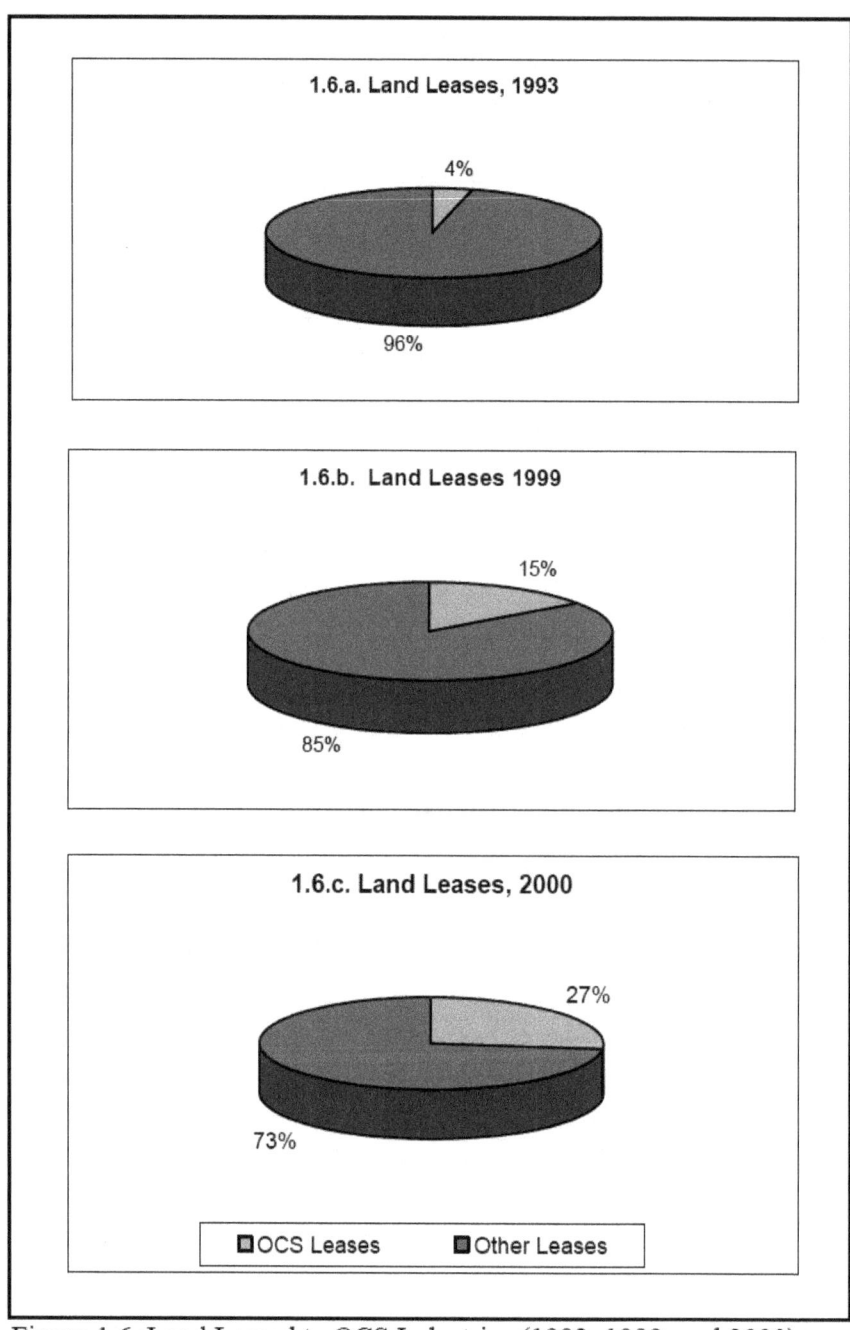

Figure 1.6. Land Leased to OCS Industries (1993, 1999, and 2000), Port of Galveston.

The development trends of OCS activities at the Port of Galveston clearly indicate the market adjustments made by the service providers. Overall, the OCS service sector at the Port of Galveston has expanded its capacity during the last decade and is poised to serve the increasing demand for services in the WPA. However, the development plans identified by Edison Chouest and Cooper-Cameron Corporation for industry expansion are behind schedule with no substantial progress as originally envisaged.

1.5.3. Long-term Industry Adjustments

Several macroeconomic indicators were analyzed examine whether the slow development of OCS activities at the port are due to long-term structural changes in the industry. A trend analysis of state personal incomes in Texas and Louisiana indicated that the state economies grew at 4.5 percent/yr in Louisiana and by 7.2 percent in Texas (Table 1.6). However, during this period of positive economic growth for both states, the numbers employed in the oil and gas industry in Texas declined by 3,600persons/yr, while Louisiana registered a modest increase of 300 persons/yr. These macroeconomic conditions may partially explain the slow development of offshore activities at the Port of Galveston.

Table 1.6

Number Employed in Oil and Gas Industry – Louisiana and Texas, 1992-2000

Annual Growth Rate 1992-2000	Louisiana	Texas
	(percent/yr)	
Number Employed in Oil and Gas Industry	0.3	-3.6
State Personal Income	4.5	7.2

Source: U.S. Bureau of Labor Statistics (Website: http://www.bls.gov).

1.6. Conclusions

The offshore service activities performed at four GOM ports are examined in this report. Increased demand for port services associated with the rapid expansion of OCS activities in the 1990's is evident from the adjustments made by the individual ports. Given that these trends are projected to continue, public infrastructure planning to accommodate OCS growth will be a priority at these ports.

2. Ports and the OCS Supply Network

2.1. Introduction

An effective logistical support system linking offshore installations with onshore supply bases is vital for deepwater oil and gas exploration. The OCS supply network operates as an intermodal transportation system, coordinating the movement of goods and services from land-based transportation modes to offshore. In this system, ports have emerged as important supply bases connecting the onshore network with the waterborne offshore segment. In addition to cargo handling, ports also serve as industrial sites for large shipyards, equipment fabrication and repair, and value-added processing activities for both inputs and outputs of the industry.

Furthermore, public port authorities effectively serve the offshore oil and gas industry in two other important areas. Ports play a leading role in influencing the community's and the industry's use of infrastructure at the port. The acceptance gained by public port authorities as non-profit agencies engaged in economic development assists in shaping community attitudes in favor of the oil and gas industry. As the rapid expansion of OCS activities has imposed pressures on limited public facilities at some ports, this issue is vital to the industry.

Public ports, acting as a conduit for inflows of low-cost public capital, provide an element of subsidy to the oil and gas industry. The port infrastructure, financed from federal and state grants and local taxes, are leased to OCS service providers below market costs.

2.2. Study Approach and Outline

The main focus of this study is to 1) analyze and define the nature of port services supporting deepwater oil and gas exploration, and 2) estimate demand and supply adjustments of the industry in the 1990's with the opening up of OCS areas for oil and gas exploration. For this purpose, a database on port activities was developed for four major ports in the GOM (Port Fourchon, Port of Morgan City, and Port of Iberia, Louisiana, and Port of Galveston, Texas), incorporating data on historical growth, physical facilities, capacity constraints, investment activities, etc. Using empirical data, supply and demand estimates were developed for several port activity variables. Based on the parameter estimates derived from the econometric models, growth forecasts were made through 2010. The information derived from these models may assist ports in their planning and investment decisions.

Empirical estimates could not be developed for some ports (Port of Iberia and Port of Galveston) because of data constraints. In these cases, information on port operations, infrastructure expansion trends, and financial performance were analyzed to make qualitative growth assessments. To provide detailed insights on individual operations, several case studies of private sector investment plans and operations were also included.

The Data - The data used throughout this report can be divided into two categories as offshore oil and gas industry data and data specific to each port.

Time-series data on industry variables - Time-series data on several industry activity variables for 1992-2001-period are used in the study. (1) The number of deepwater wells drilled in the GOM is used as a proxy for offshore industry expansion. The number of wells are further categorized into three as exploratory wells drilled (wells drilled for exploration), the number of development wells drilled (subset of exploratory wells identified for development and production), and the total number of wells (sum of exploratory and development wells). (2) The number of pipeline miles approved as additions to the existing offshore pipeline network is also used as an industry variable since it generates large cargo volumes. (3) In addition to the above, the number of Exploration Plans (EP) and the number of Development Operations Coordination Document (DOCD) filed by the industry (filing these two documents projecting deepwater activity levels is a statutory requirement) were also used in the empirical models for Morgan City. In estimating demand for port infrastructure these variables are used as exogenous variables hypothesizing a positive relationship between the two variables.

Data on individual ports - In estimating the demand for infrastructure facilities at Port Fourchon, port tonnage, truck traffic volumes on LA Hwy 1 – the main access road to the port, and barge traffic on Bayou Lafourche, the main barge route to the port are used as dependent variables. Similarly, the data on non-self-propelled vessel traffic on the Atchafalaya River from Morgan City to GOM are used for the Port of Morgan City. The activity levels at the Ports of Iberia and Galveston are defined on a qualitative basis estimated based on the financial performance data and on the basis of leasing rates of port property to offshore oil and gas service providers. The models specified and the empirical results derived are evaluated for each port in Chapter 3 to Chapter 6.

Extraneous information developed on different variables is an important source in interpreting the quantitative estimates derived from demand models. The information may be on technical relationships (e.g., exploratory wells drilled vs. the total number of wells drilled), long-term changes in structural relationships (technological developments in deepwater exploration) or significant public policy shifts (e.g., OCS Deepwater Royalty Act of 1995).

Similarly, an understanding of port procedures will be useful for correct interpretation of model results. For example, at "conventional" ports where intermodal cargo transfer is the main activity, the total revenue tonnage handled or its derivatives such as tonnage per gang-hour, crane moves per hour, etc., are used to compare port productivity for facility planning and for performance evaluation. As only revenue tonnage is included, the basic objective is to maximize the throughput while minimizing dwell time and intermediary operations. The total tonnage at offshore service ports is not tied to port revenue, and there is an element of storage for inventory control and lot consolidation in delivering supplies. This characteristic is more in line with the practices at an industrial plant. Nevertheless, consistent time-series data is a good, overall indicator to compare port activity levels.

The report is divided into five sections. Chapter 2 is an introduction to the supply network defining the major components of the system and the institutional characteristics of the public and private port system. Chapters 3-6 examine the nature of port services provided by the four ports selected for the study: Port Fourchon (Chapter 3), a major supply base for the industry providing a full range of services; the Port of Morgan City (Chapter 4), a location for large scale shipbuilding and repair services; the Port of Iberia (Chapter 5), distinct for its specialization in manufacturing prefabricated structures; and the Port of Galveston (Chapter 6), which operates as a service base for the WPA and international services

2.3. Major Components of the System

The major components of the offshore logistics system and the activities performed at each stage are illustrated in Figure 2.1. As shown in the figure, the port sector is only a part of the overall OCS logistics system; the inland transport and offshore sectors complete the system. The

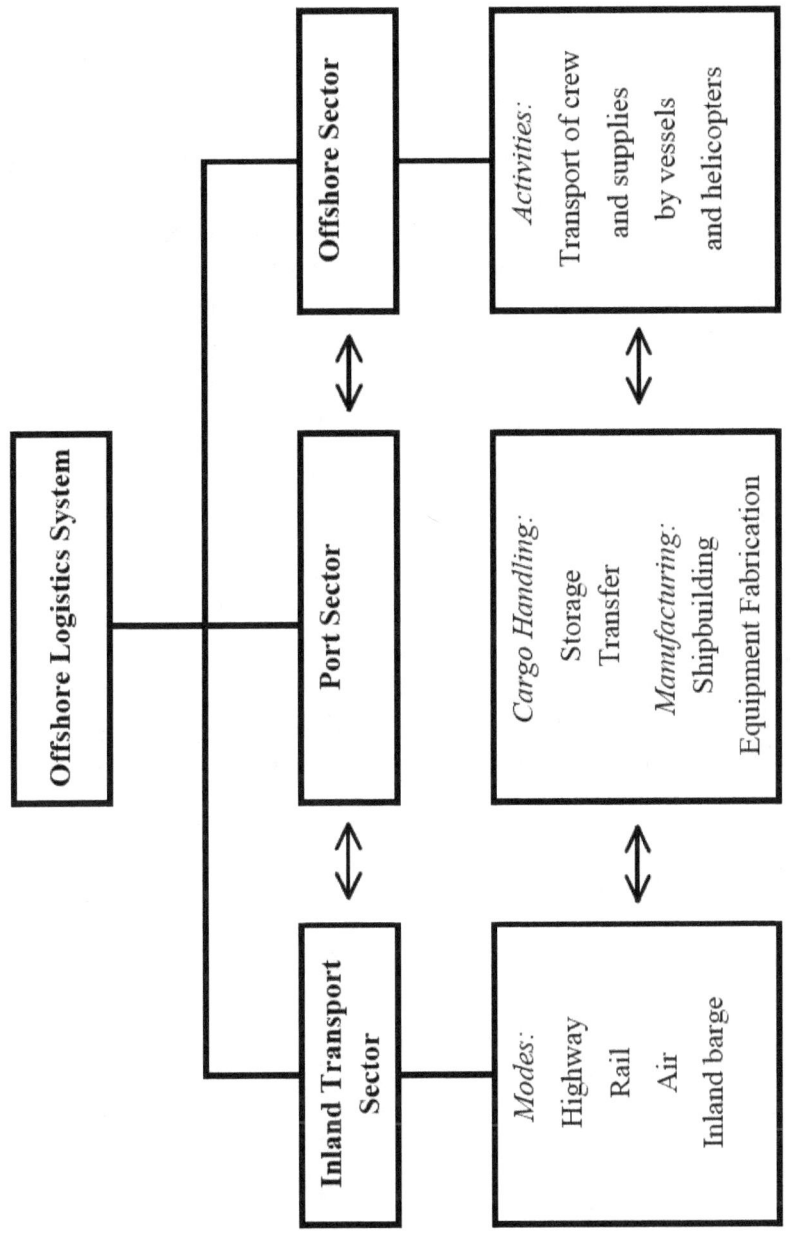

Figure 2.1. OCS Supply Network – Major Components.

overall offshore logistics system is complex, involving concepts of efficiency and productivity, inventory control, pricing, supply reliability and quality, etc. The main focus of this analysis, though, is the transportation aspects and the process of the physical movement of goods and services.

2.3.1. Inland Transport Sector

The inland transportation system consists of highways, railroads, and waterways. Trucking is the predominant mode of inland transport for supplies and pipelines for delivery of crude.

2.3.2. Offshore Sector

The vessel fleet serving the offshore sector consists of a variety of specialized vessels (anchor handling tugs, cable laying vessels, supply vessels, construction vessels, dredgers, floating storage units, shuttle tankers, mobile drilling units, mobile production systems, remotely operated vessels, standby and rescue vessels, survey vessels, and tugs). The large number of specialized offshore vessels requires berthing areas and repair and maintenance services at the port. The importance of the offshore sector is enhanced because of the large scale shipbuilding and repair industry.

2.3.3. Port Sector

A wide variety of OCS supply services are performed at ports ranging from the intermodal transfer of cargo to the fabrication, repair, and maintenance of rigs and vessels. In addition, value-added activities transpire.

Organizational Setup of the Port Sector

The organizational set up of the port network is a combination of public and private sector partnerships. The public sector ports play a pivotal role in the system by planning, constructing, and leasing public port facilities to the private sector. Differences in pricing policies and operating practices by public ports and private operators have industry-wide implications.

Public Port System

Public port authorities are political subdivisions of the State. They are managed by a board of port commissioners that are either elected or appointed to serve, usually without remuneration. Generally, port commissioners are from the local community. The organizational set-up of most of the ports reflects a desire to maintain local autonomy in business and planning decisions.

The missions and goals of public ports are to trigger economic growth and development in the local community by creating jobs and incomes, by attracting new industries, and by expanding existing industries. Predominant in their plans is the diversification of the local economy and community development, mainly through fuller utilization of local resources. As a result, the layout and facilities at most public ports resemble an industrial park as opposed to a traditional cargo handling port which encompasses storage, transfer, and transportation activities.

The principal role of public ports is to function as a 'landlord' by providing port facilities to private operators in order to generate economic activity in the community. Public ports play a dual role in the system, both as competitors and partners with the private sector enterprises. The major differences between public ports and private operators are summarized in Table 2.1.

Table 2.1

Major Characteristics of Public and Private Ports

Characteristics	Public Ports	Private Operators
Ownership and Management	Public ownership; Managed by an appointed or elected Port Commission.	Private ownership; The size of firm varies from large multi-national corporations to small businesses.
Mission and Goals	Multi-faceted public goals; Economic development, job creation and diversification of the local economy.	Business promotion motivated by profit.
Financing Methods	Grants from federal, state and local govt. agencies and self-generated funds.	Private capital
Operating Practices	"Landlord Ports"; Owns and leases basic facilities to private sector tenants.	Owns and operates, generally specializes in one service
Performance Indicators	Financial viability; volume of activities in terms of jobs created and economic development.	Financial profitability.

The partnership role of public port with the private sector involves the planning, constructing, and leasing of basic port infrastructure. By taking the initiative to invest in high-risk port expansion projects with long gestation periods, public ports limit the risk exposure of private firms. The tenants at public ports lease the facilities at subsidized rates and are exempt from paying local property taxes. Therefore, public port facilities provide an element of subsidy to the offshore logistics industry.

Offshore Service Ports – Operational Characteristics

The schematic presentation included in Figure 2.2 illustrate the typical cargo handling stages at a conventional port. Several significant differences at each stage are observed for an offshore service port:

1. *Placing trucks for unloading* - At offshore service ports, terminals are leased to different tenants engaged in specialized services. The importance of cargo transfer depends on the nature of tenant's activity, i.e., cargo transfer may be very critical for a supplier of barite but not to an operator of survey vessels. At conventional ports, all terminal operators are engaged in cargo transfer activities and throughput volumes is a general measure of terminal productivity.
2. *Moving to Warehouse from Trucks* - –At a conventional port this will be associated with exports, and again, throughput is a critical component. In

contrast, at offshore service ports this may be safety inventories that may be in storage for longer periods.

3. *Warehousing and storage* - While conventional ports attempt to maximize throughput, the functions at an offshore terminal are akin to that of an industrial plant where uninterrupted input supply and inventory control are the major concerns.

4. *Product fabrication and consolidation in the staging area* - The major logistical activities at offshore port service terminals are fabrication and assembly of equipment, storage, and consolidation of shipments. The nature of activities in this area will depend on offshore requirements in exploration, development, and production etc. At conventional ports the staging area is for loading and unloading of vessels.

5. *Stowage in vessel* - Transporting goods (personnel and cargo) offshore by either air or water is an important element of the logistical system. Common cargo items include food and provisions, water for drinking, water for industrial use, drilling mud, lubricants and fluids, waste disposal, and turbines and other instrumentation. This stage is more or less similar to both types of ports.

Coastal ports play a pivotal role in the OCS intermodal transportation system as service bases coordinating onshore and offshore segments. They provide land at the waterfront and invest in high-risk port projects in which the private sector may not be willing to invest. The public port system, with its roots in the local community, has made substantial contributions to the efficient and smooth functioning of the OCS logistical supply network.

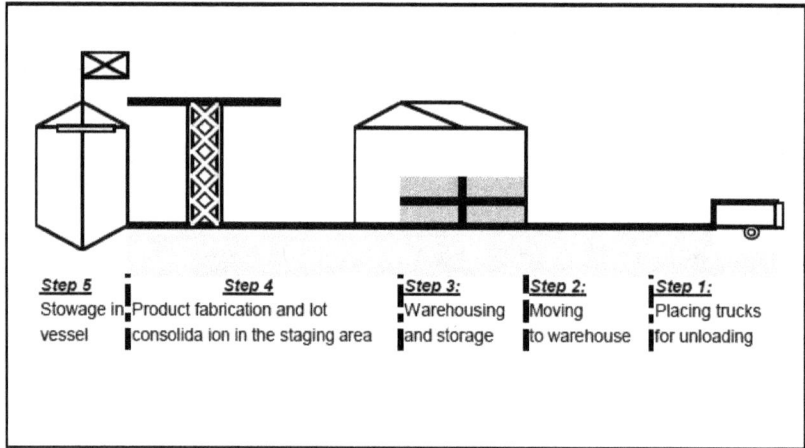

Figure 2.2. Sequence of Intermodal Cargo Transfer at Ports.

3. Port Fourchon

Port Fourchon is as the largest supply base operating in the GOM. It provides logistical support to the offshore oil and gas industry in the WPA, CPA, and EPA. The major factors favoring the Port are its central location on the GOM and the availability of first-rate public port facilities which are operated by more than 70 private sector service providers. Port Fourchon is also the homeport for the Louisiana Offshore Oil Terminal (LOOP), a terminal equipped to handle 1.2 million barrels of crude oil a day and responsible for about 13 percent of the nation's oil imports. . According to pending EP's, OCS operators have designated Port Fourchon as the service base for 44 percent of planned deepwater projects[2] (MMS, 2002). This implies that Port Fourchon's significant market share of OCS service activities will continue in the future.

3.1. Framework for Analysis

This chapter estimates the demand for port services generated by the OCS oil and gas industry supply network at Port Fourchon. It includes the following sections:

- Analysis of current port activities, historical trends, and relationships;
- Identification of databases and definition of variables;
- Empirical demand analysis for port services and forecasts; and
- Implications to public port policy planning for infrastructure.

3.2. Port Infrastructure and Operations

3.2.1. Location and Transportation Links

Port Fourchon is located on Bayou Lafourche in Louisiana. The main access channel from the Port to the GOM is Belle Pass and Bayou Lafourche. The developed area of the port is connected to the Gulf by the inshore channel in Belle Pass and Bayou Lafourche with a depth of 24 feet and a bottom width of 300 feet. The distance from the port to the Gulf (mile 0.0) is 3.4 miles and it extends another 1.3 miles maintaining -26 feet at the entrance to the Gulf. The channel is maintained by the U.S. Army Corp of Engineers. On the landside, the Port is linked to the inland waterway network through Bayou Lafourche.

The Port is connected to the State's main highway network through a two-mile segment on LA Hwy 3090 that runs from the port to LA Hwy 1, and a 40-mi segment on LA Hwy 1 to US Hwy 90. Excessive roadway flooding, older two-lane mechanical lift-span bridge at Leesville, two-lane undivided roadway are identified as the major constraints resulting in congestion, delay, incidents and excessive travel times on this segment of the highway. Among the major improvements planned are to construct a two or four-lane elevated highway structure from Fourchon to Golden Meadow, construct a four-lane fixed span bridge over the Gulf Intracoastal Waterway and Bayou Lafourche at Larose, and widen and upgrade LA Hwy 1 from Grand Isle to Fourchon.

The cost of above improvements were estimated to be about $929.6 million in 1999[3], and several methods of financing from local, state and federal sources as well as user-tolls are under consideration.

---

[2] *Deepwater Gulf of Mexico 2002: America's Expanding Frontier, (MMS, 2002)*
[3] *Preliminary Implementation Plan for the OCS Intermodal Corridor, (URS Grenier Clyde, 1999).*

3.2.2. Port Infrastructure

In addition to OCS activities, Port Fourchon serves as an important location for outdoor recreation such as recreational fishing and commercial fishing and boating. Several companies that serve the fishing industry, repairing and maintaining yachts and boats are located at the port. Recreational vessel traffic on the Bayou Lafourche and Bell Pass waterways are high during summer and weekends.

Port Facilities - Infrastructure at the Port consists of three major components. The basic port facilities, such as waterfront land, access slips, and bulkheads, are built by the public port and leased to private operators. Cranes, fork-loaders, storage tanks, and transit sheds necessary for individual operations are supplied by the private sector tenants. Service vessels which carry supplies and crew offshore are also private sector operations. Various degrees of vertical integration, though, are evident in delivering services (i.e., vessel operators controlling supplies and other types of functional coordination).

The Greater Lafourche Port Commission has made significant investments to expand public port facilities during the last 12 years. Under the Louisiana Port Construction and Development Priority Program (PCDP), more than $49 million have been invested to construct a 17,000 linear-ft bulkhead and improve 300 ac of additional waterfront land (Figure 3.1).

A 1999 survey, conducted by the port identified the following port facilities:

- 283 berths, extending 34,282 linear ft in length;
- 56 warehouses;
- 652 storage tanks; and
- 433 ac of leased waterfront land.

While the berths and waterfront land are public facilities, the warehouses and storage tanks are built and owned by private operators.

Demand for port facilities is strong despite a pricing policy to increase lease rental rates by 5 percent each year by the Port. According to Port records, tenants have made commitments two to three years in advance for the facilities that are currently under construction. As a result of increased activities and higher rental rates, Port operating revenues increased by 82 percent in four years, from $3.38 million in 1996 to $6.16 million in 2000.

All indications are that the port infrastructure facilities are currently in short supply. An aggressive investment plan to expand port facilities may be necessary to accommodate the anticipated growth in OCS oil and gas logistics services. The Port has acquired 1,700 acres to the north along the Floatation Canal for development. However, since these areas around the port are designated wetlands, the port has to incur additional costs for wetland mitigation.

3.3 Data and Definition of Variables

Time-series data available for analysis is limited; OCS oil and gas exploration activities, in its present form, started in the early 1990's. The industry also went through a rapid transformation in the 1990's which created structural changes in variable relationships. Changing government policies, developments in deepwater exploration technologies, and mergers among the majors contributed to these changes. Structural change problems in time-series data tend to make the data series discontinuous and referring virtually to different populations. Significant changes have to be expected, though, in an industry where deepwater

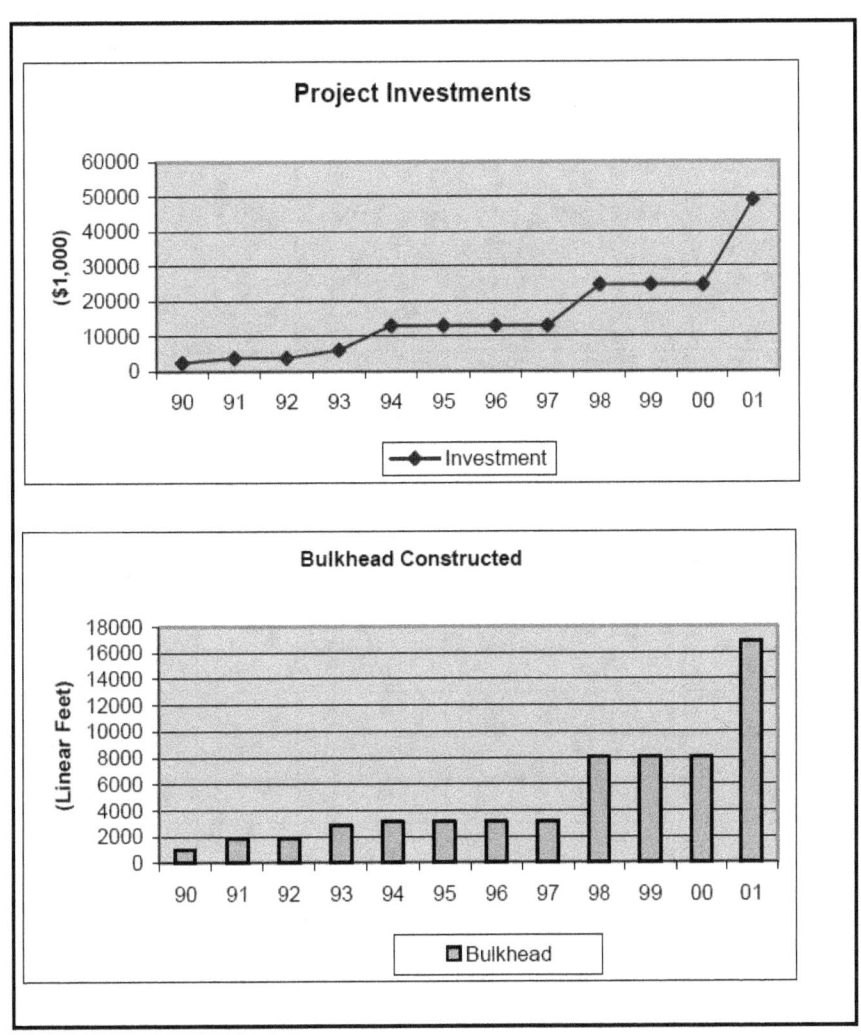

Figure 3.1. Cumulative Port Investments on Bulkhead Extensions (1990-2000).

oil production rose over 800 percent and deepwater gas production increased about 1,500 percent from 1992 to 2001. Similarly, by improving system efficiencies, the lag from leasing to production for deepwater fields has been reduced from 6.68 years in 1990 to 1.72 years in 2001.

The data used in estimating the demand for port services at Port Fourchon is included in Table 3.1. While columns 1 through 4 represent OCS variables, columns 5 through 10 represent Port activity variables. Since the changes made in the method of categorizing the time-series data is not consistent over time, the data on development wells drilled (MMS, 2002; p. 50) is not used in the analysis. The oil and gas industry variables selected (the number of OCS wells drilled and the miles of planned oil and gas pipelines) are considered to be directly related to supply logistics and relevant to estimate the market demand for port services.

The total tonnage handled at the port, truck traffic counts on the main port access road (LA Hwy 1), and the barge traffic volumes on the main inland channel (Bayou Lafourche) are selected as variables indicating port activity-levels. While the three variables are somewhat related to each other, the analysis of traffic and growth relationships and tonnage will provide unique information useful for infrastructure planning decisions. Improved port access is thought to be particularly important for OCS service ports that are located away from large urban centers.

Table 3.1

Data Series on OCS- and Port-Related Variables

	Number of OCS Wells Drilled			New Pipeline	Trucks on LA Hwy 1 South	Galliano Bridge	Fuel	Water	Bulk /Gen	Total
Year	Dev. Well (1)	Expl. Wells (2)	Total (3)	Miles (4)	# Trips /Year (5)	# of Openings (6)	Mil. Tons (7)	Mil. Tons (8)	Mil. Tons (9)	Mil. Tons (10)
1992	27	7	34	76	**	**	**	**	**	3.900
1993	29	12	41	52	**	4.188	**	**	**	4.900
1994	37	28	65	193	87,235	4,383	**	**	**	6.800
1995	51	34	85	139	98,550	4,492	**	**	**	7.300
1996	71	42	113	329	116,435	4,599	0.453	2.261	6.278	8.992
1997	88	84	172	285	144,175	4,623	0.219	2.040	8.827	11.086
1998	57	112	169	450	146,365	5,089	0.511	2.511	12.989	16.011
1999	49	123	172	512	151,110	4,643	0.510	3.740	15.521	19.501
2000	67	146	213	241	168,630	5,218	0.693	3.527	20.992	25.212
2001	60	148	208	711	211,335	5,717	0.882	3.856	22.738	27.207

Notes on data sources:
1. Data in columns 1, 2, 3, and 4 are from *Deepwater Gulf of Mexico 2002: America's Expanding Frontier* (MMS, 2002).
2. Data in columns 5 to 10 are from the databases maintained by the Greater Lafourche Port Commission.

3.3.1. Historical Trends

An analysis of historical trends and the nature of variable relationships included in Table 3.1 are appropriate before the empirical demand analysis.

Truck Traffic Trends

The trends of truck traffic with the number of OCS wells drilled and with the miles of pipeline approved for the period 1992 to 2001 are illustrated in Figure 3.2a. While the trend lines for the total number of wells drilled and truck traffic closely follow each other, the pipeline approvals as presented indicate wide annual variations. However, the trend lines for the variables indicate similar growth patterns.

Barge Traffic Trends

The barge traffic trends are compared with the oil and gas industry variables in Figure 3.2b.

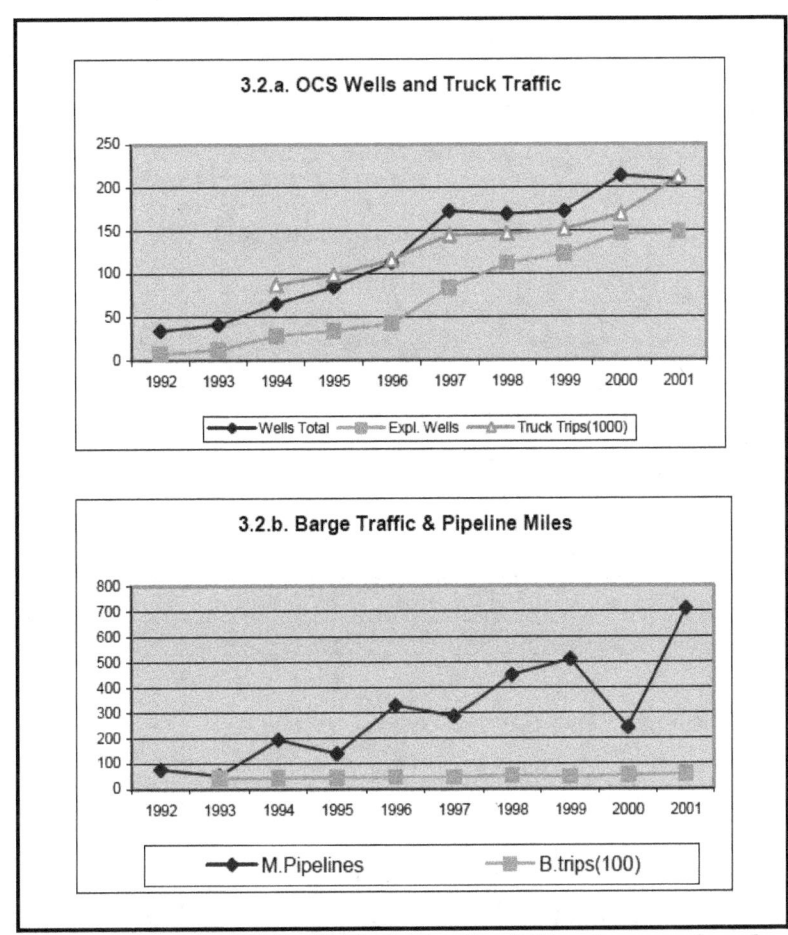

Figure 3.2. OCS Wells Drilled, Pipeline Miles Approved, and
Truck, and Barge Traffic Trends.

Port Tonnage Trends and Seasonal Variations

As mentioned earlier, port tonnage is an important indicator useful for comparing port performance and for infrastructure planning. The cargo-handling trend for Port Fourchon during the ten-year period 1992-2001 is shown in Figure 3.3. The total tonnage database can be desegregated into three major cargo categories: fuel supplies, water supplies, and dry cargo (bulk, general, and container cargo) for the last six years. During the period 1992-2001, the general and bulk cargo handled increased by more than six times, and during the period 1996-2001 the demand for water and fuel grew by 70 and 90 percent respectively. A marked increase in annual rates of growth in total tonnage is observed since 1997.

Analysis of Port Tonnage for Seasonal Variations and by Cargo Type

As port capacity requirements are directly related to peak activity periods, the seasonal distribution patterns of the tonnages handled at Port Fourchon were analyzed by commodity type. Monthly tonnage data is included in Appendix A, Table A.1.2.

In order to make a comparative analysis between cargo types, coefficients of variation were computed. Coefficient of variation is a standardized measure derived by dividing the mean of the dataset by the standard deviation. The seasonal variability for fuel and cargo tonnage is lower than the demand variability for water and crew transport, requiring the latter two sectors to carry excess capacities to meet peak requirements (Table 3.2). The peak periods for bulk and general cargo are shown as deviations from the mean in Figure 3.4. The seasonal trends for other commodities more or less indicate similar patterns.

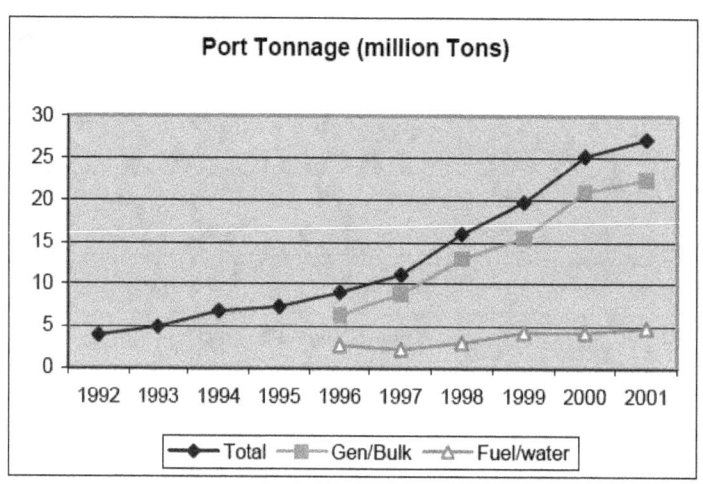

Figure 3.3. Port Tonnage Trends.

Table 3.2

Monthly Variations in Cargo Handled (1996-2000 Average)

Month	General/Bulk Cargo (tons)	Fuel (tons)	Water (tons)	Crew Change (# persons)
Total	12,867,697	477,021	2,815,966	163,326
Mean	1,072,308	36,597	234,664	13,611
Range	387,406	13,690	194,132	6,954
Standard Deviation	127,633	3,599	47,761	2,066
Coefficient of Variation	11.9%	9.83%	20.4%	15.2%

Source: Appendix A, Table A.1.2.

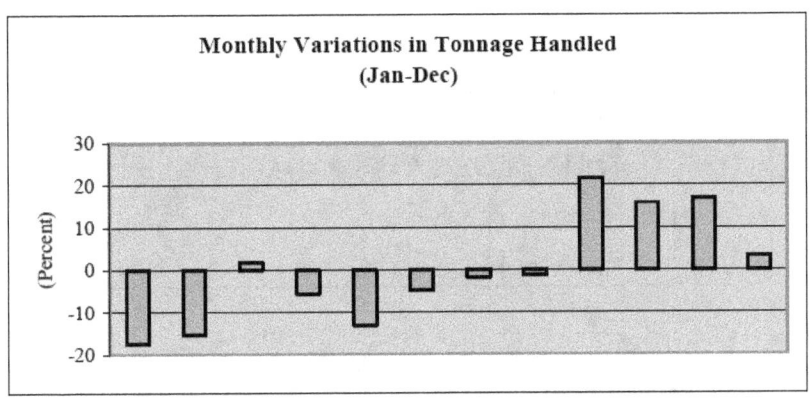

Figure 3.4. Monthly Variations for Bulk Cargo (1996-2000 Average).

3.4. Estimating the Demand for Port Services

3.4.1. Model Specification

The basic assumption a priory in specifying models is that changes in oil and gas exploration activities lead to changes in demand for port services. Since the demand for port services is derived from the aggregate logistics demand for the industry, this relationship is intuitively obvious. Two datasets, the number of OCS wells drilled and the number of oil and gas pipelines approvals, are used as proxy variables to represent the changes in activity levels in the oil and gas industry (see Table 3.1). The number of wells drilled is positively related to the cargo volumes generated in the logistics network in terms of industry inputs as well as to industry outputs of oil and gas. The increase in pipeline extensions generates substantial cargo volumes as an activity itself and the demand for network extension signify growth in terms of spatial distribution and increase output volumes. These are treated as exogenous (explanatory) variables generating the demand for port services. Selected port activities such as inland traffic volumes on access roads and channels, and port tonnage that utilize public port facilities are used as dependent variables responding to the demand for port services.

A schematic of the models specified and the variable relationships are shown in (Figure 3.5). Based on the dataset in Table 3.1, three exogenous and three endogenous variables were identified for model specification. Nine single equation regression models (3x3) each with a unique variable relationship were specified to examine the demand for trucking, barge transport, and for cargo tonnage handled at the port. The choice of statistical technique was dictated by data limitations and other characteristics in variable relationships. Single equation regression models were specified to estimate the relationship between truck traffic and the number of OCS wells drilled. Single equation regressions with lagged explanatory variables were used to estimate the relationships between port activity variables and pipeline approvals because of the time lag between them. The lag model for estimating truck traffic in LA Hwy 1 (Model 1.3), for example, will use time-series data on pipeline approvals from 1992-1999 and the truck traffic data from 1994-2001 in the models pairing each observation of the independent variable with a two-year lag dependent variable.

Independent Variables
4. Total Number of OCS Wells Drilled
5. Number of OCS Exploratory Wells Drilled
6. Number of Pipeline Miles Approved

Dependent Variables
4. Number of Trucks South Bound on LA Hwy 1
5. Number of Galliano Bridge Openings
6. Total Tons at Port

Regression Models		
Model Number	**Independent Variable**	**Dependent Variable**
1.1	Total OCS Wells Drilled	Trucks South Bound on LA Hwy 1
1.2	Exploratory Wells Drilled	Trucks South Bound on LA HWY 1
1.3	Pipeline Miles Approved	Trucks South Bound on LA HWY 1
2.1	Total OCS Wells Drilled	Galliano Bridge Openings
2.2	Exploratory Wells Drilled	Galliano Bridge Openings
2.3	Pipeline Miles Approved	Galliano Bridge Openings
3.1	Total OCS Wells Drilled	Total Port Tonnage
3.2	Exploratory Wells Drilled	Total Port Tonnage
3.3	Pipeline Miles Approved	Total Port Tonnage

Figure 3.5. Model Specification and Variable Relationships Estimated.

3.4.2. Truck Traffic Demand

Based on historical data from 1994 to 2001, the demand for truck traffic was estimated using three regressions models where the truck traffic on LA HWY 1 is the dependent variable and the three independent variables as shown in Figure 3.2a. A summary of all model estimates derived is shown in Table 3.3, and the detailed specifications of all models and the computer output are included as Appendix A. The numbering method for models is to identify by them by the number of the dependent and independent variable respectively.

Truck Traffic Demand and Total Number of OCS Wells Drilled (Model 1:1)

The number of wells drilled is assumed to be the causal variable driving the demand for logistic services and the truck traffic is a proxy for port services. The linear regression model specified is of the form:

$$Y = a + bX,$$

where Y represents truck traffic volumes on LA HWY 1 and a and b are the intercept term and the regression coefficient respectively. Using each independent variable mentioned above, three demand models were estimated.

The regression model estimating the relationship between total OCS wells drilled and truck traffic (Regression Model 1.1) indicates strong, positive correlation with 85 percent of the variation ($R^2 = 0.87$) in truck traffic being explained by the model (Table 3.3). The regression coefficient, the intercept term, and F-values are statistically significant. According to the regression coefficient (slope) estimate, the technical relationship between the two variables is for every OCS well drilled there is a corresponding increase in truck trips by 628/yr.

Truck Traffic Demand and the Number of OCS Exploratory Wells Drilled (Model 1.2)

The regression results indicate that the number of exploratory wells is highly correlated with truck traffic volumes with a R^2 value of 0.8648, and the other results are essentially comparable with the results derived from Regression Model 1.1. The model estimates that for every exploratory well drilled in the GOM, the truck traffic on LA HWY 1 will increase by an additional 744 trips/yr.

Number of Pipeline Miles Approved and Truck Traffic Demand (Regression Model 1.3)

Because of the time lag involved between plan approvals and the laying of pipelines, it is necessary to specify the model with lagged explanatory variables. Several regression equations were specified with lagged data on pipeline approvals as the explanatory variable and trucking data as the dependent variable. After testing successive lagged models, the model with a two-year lag (X_{t-2}) indicated statistically significant results. All parameter estimates were significant with a high R^2 value of 0.85. According to model estimates for every additional mile of pipeline extension, the truck traffic will increase by 217 trips.

Table 3.3

Regression Estimates for Truck Traffic, Barge Traffic, and Port Tonnage

Independent Variable	Model Number	Intercept	Regression Coefficient	R^2	F-Value
Truck Traffic South Bound on LA Hwy 1					
Total OCS Wells Drilled	1:1	39,817 (2.39)*	673 (6.40)*	0.87	40.98*
Exploratory Wells Drilled	2:1	73,757 (6.08*)	744 (6.20*)	0.86	38.39*
Pipeline Miles Approved (lagged by 2-year period)	3:1	85,327 (7.57*)	217 (5.76*)	0.85	33.20*
Barge Traffic at Galliano Bridge					
Total OCS Wells Drilled	1:2	3,894 (16.91*)	6.39 (4.16*)	0.71	17.30*
Exploratory Wells Drilled	2:2	4,142 (25.75*)	7.78 (4.61*)	0.75	21.28*
Pipeline Miles Approved (lagged by 2-year period)	3:2	4,207 (36.02*)	2.51 (6.44*)	0.87	41.48*
Port Tonnage					
Total OCS Wells Drilled	1:3	-1.46 (-0.59)	0.11 (6.66*)	0.85	44.39*
Exploratory Wells Drilled	2:3	2.18 (1.95**)	0.15 (11.96*)	0.95	143.53*
Pipeline Miles Approved (lagged by 2-year period)	3:3	3.64 (2.33*)	0.046 (8.79*)	0.93	77.23*

*Symbols * and ** denote statistical significance levels at 5% and 10% respectively.*
Source: Appendix A tables.

3.4.3. Inland Barge Traffic Demand

Inland Barge Traffic and Total Number of OCS Wells Drilled (Regression Model 2.1)
All parameter estimates derived from this model were statistically significant. The results indicated that for every OCS well drilled, bridge openings increase by about 7 openings.

Inland Barge Traffic and OCS Exploratory Wells Drilled (Regression Model 2.2)
The model results are more or less similar to Regression Model 2:1. The model estimates that 8 additional bridge openings will be necessary for each new exploratory well drilled in the GOM.

Inland Barge Traffic and Miles of Pipelines Approved (Regression Model 2.3)
This model specified with the number of pipeline approvals as the explanatory variable shows a strong correlation with barge traffic. All parameter estimates are statistically significant and the regression model yields an R^2 value of 0.87. The regression equation estimates that for every mile extension of oil and gas pipeline three bridge openings for barges to pass will be necessary.

3.4.4. Cargo Activities Demand

Demand for Cargo Handling and Total Number of OCS Wells Drilled (Regression Model 3:1)
The model estimates indicate a strong correlation between the two variables ($R^2 = 0.85$). The slope coefficient and F-value of the regression are statistically significant.

Demand for Cargo Handling and Number of OCS Exploratory Wells Drilled (Regression Model 3:2)
According to model estimates, these two variables provide the 'best fit' with an R^2 value of 0.95 and an F-value of 143.5. According to model estimates, for each additional OCS well drilled, port tonnage will increase by 114,500 tons; for each exploratory well, port tonnage will increase by 148,500 tons.

Demand for Cargo Handling and Miles of Pipelines Approved (Regression Model 3.3)
The demand relationship between these two variables was estimated using regression analysis with a lagged independent variable. The model estimates from the two-year lag model (X_{t-2}) were statistically significant with a R^2 value of 0.93. For every additional extension of the pipeline network by one mile, port tonnage increase by 45,000 tons.

Port Cargo Tonnage Handled by Type of Cargo
Using the tonnage data by cargo type, several models were specified to estimate the demand for water, fuel, and general/bulk cargo. The model specification used the tonnages of the three commodities as the dependent variables and the independent variables remained the same as described above. All models yielded statistically significant results; the computer output is included in Appendix A (Regression Models 4.1-4.9).

31

3.5. Demand Forecasts

3.5.1. Forecasting Approach

Based on the model estimates described above, forecasts were made for trucking, inland barge traffic, and cargo handling trends at the port. For each activity, three alternative estimates were made with 2010 as the forecast horizon. The following three-step procedure was adopted in developing the forecasts.

The future growth rates for the three independent variables (total number of OCS wells drilled, the exploratory wells drilled, and the number of pipeline approvals) were determined by trend extrapolation of historical data from 1992 to 2001. The trend extrapolation results for the variables are shown in Appendix A, Table A.1.4. The rates of annual growth for the three variables are shown in Table 3.4. For example, the total number wells drilled increases at an annual rate of 21.92 during the period;

The regression coefficient estimates derived from individual models (Table 3.3) were applied to the trend line estimates to derive annual rates of growth in each activity and the final forecasts were developed through 2010 using the actual data for 2001 as the baseline (Table 3.5).

Table 3.4

Technical Relationships between Variables: Estimated Annual Growth Rates
for Truck Traffic, Barge Traffic, and Port Tonnage

Independent Variables	Rate of Annual Growth of Independent Variable	Truck Traffic Growth (# trips)		Barge Traffic (# trips)		Port Tonnage (millions)	
		Per Unit	Annual	Per Unit	Annual	Per Unit	Annual
Total wells drilled	21.92	627.8	13,761	6.39	140	0.115	2.52
Exploratory wells drilled	17.93	744.4	13,347	7.78	139	0.149	2.51
Pipeline miles approved	57.71	216.71	12,506	2.51	145	0.0458	2.64

3.5.2. Growth Projections

Truck Traffic Forecasts

The demand forecasts for trucking estimated through 2010 using the above procedure are shown in Table 3.5. The point estimates made for trucking by the three models are highly consistent, with a median forecast of 331,400 trucks in 2010 and the highest and the lowest forecasts falling within two percent of the median forecast. A technical evaluation of the above estimates using statistical comparisons for forecasting accuracy is beyond the purview of this report. According to the median forecast, truck traffic is expected to grow at an annual rate of 5 percent and the overall growth for the nine-year period is about 60 percent. The three trucking trends are illustrated in Figure 3.6a.

Table 3.5

Truck Traffic, Barge Traffic, and Tonnage Forecasts Using Three Alternative Models

Year	Truck Traffic (1000)			Barge Traffic			Port Tonnage (million tons)		
	Model 1.1	Model 1.2	Model 1.3	Model 2.1	Model 2.2	Model 2.3	Model 3.1	Model 3.2	Model 3.3
2001*	211.3	211.3	211.3	5,717	5,717	5,717	27.207	27.207	27.207
2002	225.1	224.7	223.8	5,857	5,856	5,862	29.727	29.717	29.847
2003	238.9	238.0	236.3	5,997	5,995	6,007	32.247	32.227	32.487
2004	252.6	251.4	248.8	6,137	6,134	6,152	34.767	34.737	35.127
2005	266.4	264.7	261.3	6,277	6,273	6,297	37.287	37.247	37.767
2006	280.1	278.1	273.8	6,417	6,412	6,442	39.807	39.757	40.407
2007	293.9	291.4	286.3	6,557	6,551	6,587	42.327	42.267	43.047
2008	307.6	304.8	298.8	6,697	6,690	6,732	44.847	44.777	45.687
2009	321.4	318.1	311.3	6,837	6,829	6,877	47.367	47.287	48.327
2010	335.2	331.4	323.9	6,977	6,968	7,022	49.887	49.797	50.967

*Figures for 2001 are actual numbers.

Barge Traffic Forecasts

The three barge traffic forecasts are very consistent with only a small variation between forecasts. The overall growth rate is about 22 percent for the period with 2-3 percent annual growth. The trends of growth for barge traffic are illustrated in Figure 3.6b.

Port Tonnage Forecasts

The median cargo forecast of 50 million tons in 2010 represents an overall increase of about 100 percent or doubling of the volume. In terms of annual growth, it amounts to about 7-8 percent. The three forecasts have a variation of less than 2 percent from the median forecast. The cargo forecasts are illustrated in Figure 3.6c.

Port Tonnage Forecast by Cargo Type

The cargo tonnage was desegregated and forecasts were made for water, fuel, and general/bulk cargo. The model results (Models 1.4 to Model 3.6) and the forecasts are included in Appedix C.

3.6. Structural Analysis and Policy Implications

Correlation Between Variables

The correlation matrix for the ten variables included in this analysis is shown in Table 3.6. The industry variables are in columns 1 to 4 and the port activity variables are in columns 5 to 10. Overall, both variables (the number of wells drilled and the miles of pipeline approvals),

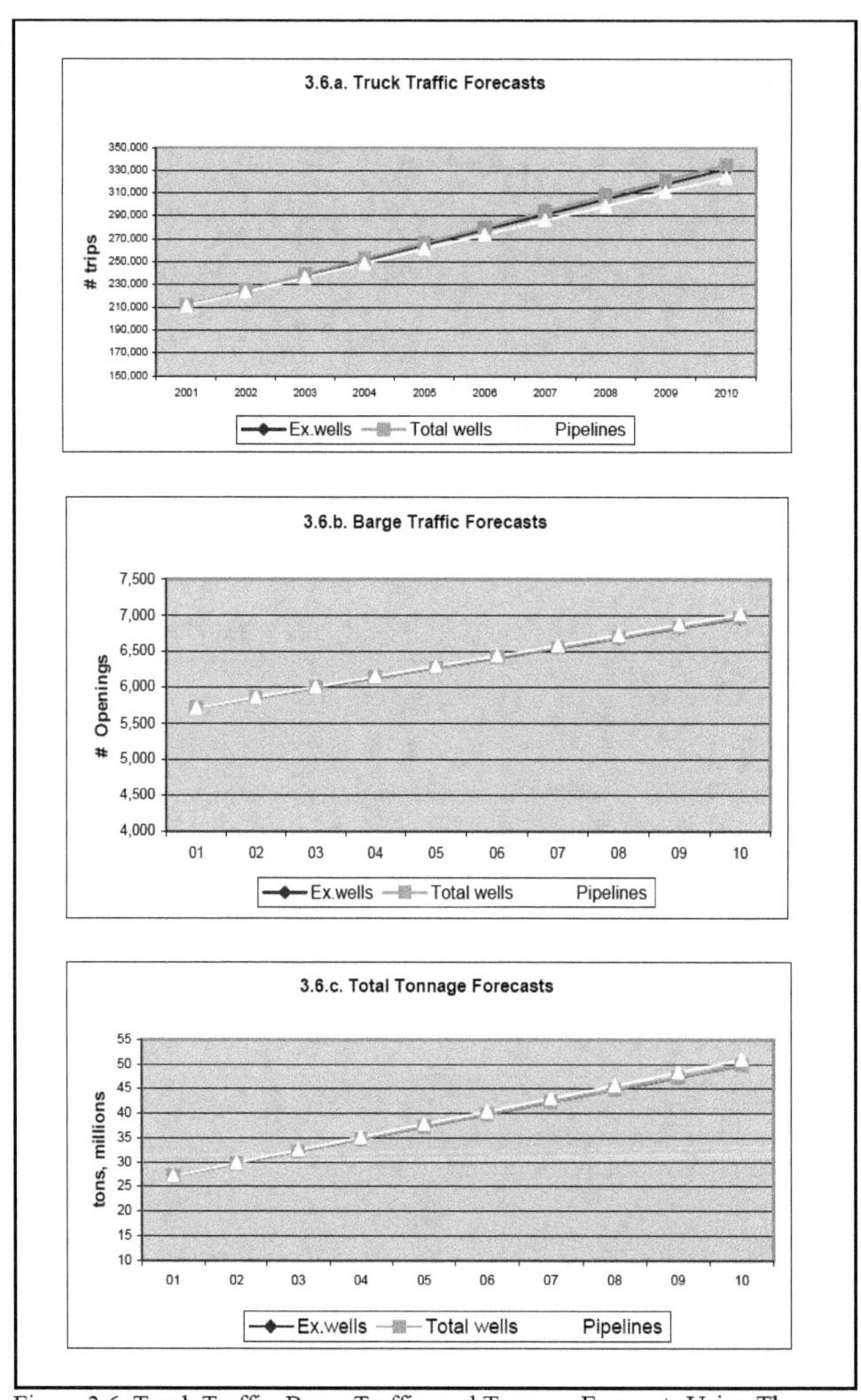

Figure 3.6. Truck Traffic, Barge Traffic, and Tonnage Forecasts Using Three Alternative Models.

34

Table 3.6

Correlation Matrix for Analysis Variables – Port Fourchon

	Column 1	Column 2	Column 3	Column 4	Column 5	Column 6	Column 7	Column 8	Column 9	Column 10
Column 1	1.0000									
Column 2	0.5522	1.0000								
Column 3	0.7333	0.9718	1.0000							
Column 4	0.4331	0.7982	0.7735	1.0000						
Column 5	0.3460	0.9300	0.9340	0.7983	1.0000					
Column 6	0.3966	0.8675	0.8437	0.7801	0.9138	1.0000				
Column 7	-0.5662	0.7101	0.5890	0.6105	0.7993	0.8829	1.0000			
Column 8	-0.6895	0.8265	0.6741	0.5740	0.7461	0.5973	0.8128	1.0000		
Column 9	-0.4831	0.9575	0.8998	0.4818	0.9014	0.8361	0.8631	0.8910	1.0000	
Column 10	0.4482	0.9732	0.9205	0.7913	0.9326	0.9027	0.8743	0.9136	0.9985	1.0000

Notes:

Column 1 - Number of OCS development wells   Column 6 - Number of Galliano bridge openings

Column 2 - Number of OCS exploratory wells   Column 7 - Fuel tonnage

Column 3 - Total number of OCS wells   Column 8 - Water tonnage

Column 4 - Miles of pipelines approved   Column 9 - General/bulk cargo tonnage

Column 5 - Annual truck traffic on LA Hwy 1   Column 10 - Total port tonnage

representing the rate of industry expansion, are positively correlated with the port activity variables, confirming the theoretical economic relationships. Note that the development wells data could not be used in the analysis.

Future Forecasts

The three trucking models, as well as the three barge models, provided statistically significant parameter estimates and consistent forecasts through 2010. The high correlation between these variables is evident from the values in Table 3.6. More or less similar results were derived from the models that estimated port tonnage. Therefore, these variables could be used for forecasting the demand for port services, infrastructure planning and investment decisions.

It is important to note several assumptions implicit in estimating variable relationships. The analysis assumes the Port to be a major player in the OCS supply network, and the database accounts for those services. Another far-reaching assumption implicit in using historical data and trend extrapolation is that variable relationships and the rates of growth will continue during the forecast period. All industry variables such as new discoveries of oil and gas reserves, innovative new production systems, and the technological developments indicate a period of sustained growth for the industry. However, after the initial phases of deepwater oil and gas exploration, with maturity of the industry, it is very likely that the variable relationships for port services will change. According to the forecasts developed in this study, the tonnage at Port Fourchon will more than double by 2010 and the truck and barge traffic will increase by more than 50 percent. Therefore, a plan for upgrading public infrastructure such as highways, ports, potable water and sewerage services is a prerequisite to accommodate the high rates of industry growth and for regional development.

4. Port of Morgan City

Morgan City is an important onshore supply base currently serving several deepwater oil and gas installations. However, the shipbuilding and repair activities are of much more significance to the OCS logistics system. Most of the offshore structures served by service providers from Morgan City are located to the west of Port Fourchon, suggesting that proximity of Morgan City via the Atchafalaya River may have influenced the selection. In addition, however, business connections and historical relationships also play a role in the selection of service bases. According to the preferences indicated by the oil and gas industry operators in their pending plans filed with the MMS, Morgan City will continue to grow as a service base in the future[4].

The shipbuilding and repair services at Morgan City are of much more strategic importance to the OCS logistics network than the routine supply services. The design and construction of larger, more economical vessels that can withstand extreme weather conditions is an integral part of deepwater oil and gas exploration technology. The cost-savings brought about by construction of vessels with higher technical capabilities and the conversion of existing vessels to meet the new needs are vital to the industry.

The analysis of OCS supply activities to follow will consist of several sections. The analysis will first define the location and transportation links of the supply base. The next two sections will analyze the public port activities and the private sector operations. In the last section an empirical analysis of technical relationships between oil and gas industry variables and port activity variables will be included. These relationships will be estimated using quantitative techniques, and the results will be analyzed along with policy implications.

4.1. Location and Transportation Infrastructure

The service providers at Morgan City include the public port, the Morgan City Harbor and Terminal District, as well as private sector shipbuilders catering to the local, national and international markets. These shipyards are located mainly along the Atchafalaya River and the Gulf Intracoastal Waterway in the communities of Franklin, Morgan City, Patterson, Bayou Vista, Berwick, Amelia, and Baldwin. In general, the area including the public port and private offshore operators located in the above communities will be identified as the Morgan City supply base.

Navigable Waterways

The strategic location of the supply base at the intersection of busy navigable waterways has contributed to the development of shipbuilding and repair industries in the area. Each of the following waterway segments provides specific advantages to Morgan City (Table 4.1).

1. *Atchafalaya River, Morgan City to GOM* - Morgan City is on the Lower Atchafalaya River 18 mi from the open waters of the GOM. The navigational channel maintained by the United States Army Corps of Engineers (COE) at a depth of 20 ft. and a minimum width of 400 ft provides easy access to large offshore structures and vessels. Currently, the COE has undertaken preliminary studies to examine the feasibility of deepening the channel to 35 ft.

---

[4] The projected market shares are 44 percent for Port Fourchon, 19 percent for Venice, and 37 percent for other Gulf of Mexico ports including Morgan City, (MMS 2002; pp. 27-28).

2. *Atchafalaya River, Old River Lock to Morgan City* – This segment of the waterway provides easy access to the Mid-West via the Upper Mississippi, enabling barge transportation of major supply items such as steel plates and iron and steel piping for the offshore oil and gas industry and the shipbuilding industry.

3. *Gulf Intracoastal Waterway, Morgan City-Port Allen Route* – The industries in Morgan City area are connected to the operations on the Lower Mississippi including foreign commerce and the barge transportation network on the Mississippi.

4. *Gulf Intracoastal Waterway, Mississippi River to Sabine River* – This segment of the waterway coupled with the Atchafalaya provides a shorter route for cargo with origins and destinations in Texas and western Louisiana and the Midwest. For example, traffic between points in southeast Texas and the Upper Mississippi River Valley saves approximately 342 mi per round trip by using the Atchafalaya River rather than the alternate link of the Intracoastal via the Harvey Locks at New Orleans.

Table 4.1

Waterways Network and Traffic (2000)

Waterway Segment	Length (miles)	Depth (feet)	Freight Traffic (1,000 tons)	Vessel Trips
Atchafalaya R. Morgan City to GOM	18	20	2,740	11,628
Atchafalaya R. Morgan City to Old R. Lock	123	12	13,441	12,764
GIWW- Morgan City-Port Allen Route	64	9	23,061	15,265
GIWW- Mississippi R. to Sabine R.	266	10-12	62,855	66,805

Source: *Waterborne Commerce of the United States* (U.S. Army Corps of Engineers, 2001)

Highways

The Morgan City supply base is located on the U.S. Highway 90, which is the future corridor of I-49. The metropolitan cities of New Orleans, Baton Rouge and Lafayette are within a seventy-mile radius. Through these cities the port can access Interstates 49, 55, and 59 North and Interstate 10 East and West.

4.2. The Public Port

4.2.1. Port Organization, Location, and Facilities

The Port of Morgan City was created by Act 530 in the State Legislature in 1952. Since 1957, it has been active in both domestic and international trade. A nine member Board of Commissioners appointed by the Governor is responsible for the management. The commissioners serve on a voluntary basis with no remuneration. Each commissioner serves for a nine-year term. In the early 1990's the Port made a decision to be an operating port and started developing port facilities.

The Public port is on the east bank of the Atchafalaya River in a natural wide and deep harbor known as Berwick Bay. As discussed above, the port has benefited from its central location with close proximity to the GOM and several heavy traffic inland waterway segments. The Port of Morgan City is located 1.1 mi from U.S. Highway 90, with Lafayette 71 mi to the West on Highway 90, New Orleans 68 mi to the East and Baton Rouge 71 mi to the North. The port is served by the Burlington Northern – Santa Fe Railroad (BNSF) and provides railcar-shunting services on a daily basis.

Public Port Facilities

The public port site has a total of 28.6 ac with 22.49 ac located inside the COE floodwall and 6.11 ac located between the floodwall and Bayou Boeuf. The limited availability of land at the waterfront could constrain future port expansion plans.

The port has been able to compete successfully for funding for infrastructure improvements through the PCDP. Since 1990 the port has been awarded $9.75 million for eight projects. These projects have provided a dock, warehousing, cargo-handling equipment, rail spur, transit shed, truck yard and a rail car conveyor system (Table 4.2). The wharf area at the port has approximately 80,000 ft^2 and is used exclusively for docking and loading/unloading cargo to and from vessels. With a dock length of 800 linear-ft and 20-ft draft channel, the port is geared to handle medium-sized cargo vessels. Other facilities at the port include a 20,000 sq. ft. warehouse, a large marshalling yard, and adequate rail siding facilities. Specific port cargo handling equipment includes: a dock side mobile crane capable of lifting a fully loaded (70,000 lb) 40 ft container; three forklifts: one 8,000 lb and one 10,000 lb for warehouse use, and one 15,000 lb for the yard; a 50-ton container crane with a 130-ft boom; a 35-ton cherry picker; and a 40-ton container handler.

Table 4.2

Capital Investment Program (1990-2002)

Project	Year Funded	Project Cost ($)	Project Components
Bulkhead & Dock	1990	800,000	Construct a 500ft. wharf, fender piles and dolphins
Bulkhead & Dock, Phase II	1992	2,100,000	Dock extension by 300ft. x 80ft.
Mobile crane & cargo handling equipment	1993	1,462,500	Purchase mobile crane, forklifts, and misc. equipment
Transit shed & truck yard	1995	1,410,000	Construct 20,000 sq. ft. warehouse and paved yard
Railroad spur & loading dock	1996	874,800	3500 linear ft. rail spur and siding, and 20'x200' loading dock.
Additional dockage	1998	1,143,000	Dock extension by 27ft x 447ft.
Rail transfer and storage area	1999	1,957,000	A concrete container yard and hard surface access roads
Total Investment		9,747,300	

Source: *Port Construction and Development Priority Program,* Eighth Annual Report, Louisiana Department of Transportation and Development, 2001.

4.2.2. Port Operations and Financial Performance

As an operational port, Morgan City does not have a traditional landlord relationship with tenants. Once facilities that are currently under construction are completed and as cargo-handling activities increase, the port hopes to attract a stevedoring company that will relieve the port of some of it operational responsibilities.

The main imported items handled at the port are steel products, iron and steel pipe and tubes, oil and gas field machinery, and barite (Table 4.3). Raw materials required by the shipbuilding and repair industry and equipment fabrication needs remain as the major component in port's tonnage. In addition, the port derives revenue by offering berthing facilities for vessels providing services to the off shore oil industry.

Table 4.3

Oil and Gas Industry Related Cargo (1996-2000 Average)

Cargo Category	1996-2000 Average (tons)	1996-2000 Average (%)
Oil and Gas Related		
Barite	1,750	3.3
Iron, steel sheets & pipes	1,879	3.5
Oil and gas field machinery	9,688	18.1
Fuel oils	25,48	4.8
Total (oil and gas related)	15,865	29.6
Other Cargo	37,772	70.4
Total	53,637	100

Financing of Public Ports

The summary financial indicators included in Table 4.4 emphasize several features typical to a public port. It is interesting to note that while 12 percent of the port revenue is from a self-imposed property tax on the local community, another 81 percent are federal and state grants. Port operating revenues contribute only 5 percent to total revenue, emphasizing the local community support to public ports for job creation and economic development.

4.3. Private Sector Operators

As mentioned earlier, the private sector businesses dominate the shipbuilding and repair industries in the Morgan City area. Characteristically, these industries are large, multi-plant operations specializing in building vessels for different sectors such as the cruise industry, military vessels for the navy, recreation vessels and yachts, vessels designed for research purposes, etc. The supply and repair of offshore vessels and other drilling equipment has continued to be a significant part of the industry since the 1940's. However, with the recent developments in deepwater oil and gas exploration activities, the need for larger and faster vessels has provided a new impetus to the industry.

Table 4.4

Analysis of Revenue Sources (2000)

Budget Item	2000	
	($)	(%)
Property Taxes	520,188	11.9
Federal & State Govt. Grants	3,528,987	80.8
Port Operating Revenue	227,470	5.2
Total	4,366,366	100
Total assets	17,959,543	100

Source: Annual Financial Statements, Port of Morgan City.

4.3.1. Profiles of Major Operators

The major businesses engaged in offshore related services with more than 100 employees are listed in Table 4.5. Most of the firms are multi-plant operations, and the number of employees and annual sales shown are only for the plants located in Morgan City. For example, McDermott, Inc. is a conglomerate employing 11,400 employees in more than a dozen countries with $3.4 billion in annual revenue in 2001. Similarly, Bollinger Shipyards consist of 14 plants located in Louisiana and Texas.

Table 4.5

Major Offshore Oil and Gas Service Firms

Name of Firm	Number Employed	Annual Sales (million $)	Activity
Bollinger Marine Fabricators	400	25-100	Shipbuilding & repair
Cameron Corporation	268	10-25	Oil & gas field machinery
Conrad Industries, Inc.	200	15	Boat building & repair
Gulf Craft, Inc.	130	5-10	Boat building & repair
McDermott, Inc.	2,000	100-500	Oil & gas field machinery
SMI Cos.	120	5-10	Metal products-fabricated
Superior Fabricators, Inc.	110	14	Structural metal fabricated
Swiftships Shipbuilders, LLC	245	40	Boat building & repair
Twin Bros. Marine Corp.	240	N/A	Shipbuilding & repair

The company profiles included in Table 4.6 illustrate the typical shipyard configuration operated by the private sector. Typically, shipyards are multi-plant firms catering to national and international markets. The description of facilities indicates the highly capital intensive nature of the industry. The products and services emphasize that the shipyards cater to various industrial sectors such as the cruise industry, U.S. government agencies and the military, the offshore oil and gas industry and inland barge industry, etc. The diversified market provides a hedge against downturns in any individual sector.

In addition to the large-scale industries described above, the offshore supply network consists of many smaller firms that provide specialized services and raw materials to the shipyards.

Table 4.6

Infrastructure Facilities at Selected Private Sector Shipyards

Conrad Industries, Inc.	Bollinger Marine Fabricators	McDermott International
Plant Locations		
Operates 2 plants in LA and 1 in Texas	Operates 14 shipyards, 12 in LA and two in Texas	International conglomerate; Multi-plant locations in Asia, Africa, North and South America
Products and Services		
Construction and repair of marine vessels and oil and gas equipment.	Construction and repair of marine vessels and oil and gas equipment.	Fabrication of offshore platforms, marine vessels and installing offshore pipelines
Facilities at Morgan City		
5 dry docks with lifting capacity 900-3,000 tons; Over 110,000 sq. ft. of indoor fabrication space; Over 2,000 feet of bulkhead area; Two dredged basins for vessel repair	3 dry docks with lifting capacity 1,600 to 8,100 tons; More than 60,000 sq. ft of covered space including workshops and offices; 2,000ft.of wet dock area; 17,000 sq. ft construction slab.	2 deck assembly buildings, each 400'x 800' with 8 bays and three 20-ton overhead cranes in each bay; Jacket erection area with 46 crawler cranes ranging in capacity from 40 to 350 tons; Pipe mills – 5 buildings
Recent Projects		
Pusher tug for U.S. Army; Double hull tank barge for U.S. Navy; Towboat for Corp of Engineers; FPSO living quarters for 60 persons; A warehouse barge.	Barge derrick for U.S. Army; Patrol crafts for U.S. Coast Guard; Offshore supply vessels; Lift boats; Passenger boats and dredges.	Drilling & prod. Spar for Chevron; Sub-sea development system for Conger; Pipeline systems for BP Exploration; Drilling and prod. Platform for Marathon Oil

Source: Based on marketing information provided by individual firms.

4.4. Data and Definition of Variables

The approach followed in estimating the demand for port services at Port Fourchon is inappropriate for the present analysis for several reasons:

1. *The Database* – A database maintained by the public port was available for analysis at Port Fourchon. At Morgan City, as the services are provided by the private sector, a public database on port services is not available. Because of the proprietary nature of private sector operations, it is difficult to develop an adequate database for analysis.

2. *Low Market Share* – As the market share of port services at Morgan City is relatively low, it is likely that the models may not adequately represent industry-wide changes at a macro level.

3. *The Nature of Services* – The shipbuilding and repair services at Morgan City cater to a diversified set of clients and foreign markets. It is much more difficult to delineate the effects of the OCS oil and gas industry.

4.4.1 Industry Variables and Port Activity Levels

The set of OCS oil and gas industry variables (columns 1-6) and the volumes of vessel traffic on the Atchafalaya River representing the port activity levels (columns 7-9) were selected as variables for the demand analysis (Table 4.7). While the number of wells drilled act as a proxy for industry expansion and as a quantitative measure for logistical service requirements, the number of pipeline miles approved provides an estimate of one major item of freight generated by the industry. The EP's and Development Operations Coordination Documents (DOCD) are indications of progress made by the industry in terms of individual operations. In modeling the demand for port services, these six variables are treated as exogenous variables.

Port Activity Variables

Unlike at Port Fourchon where port operations are centered at the public port, the activities at Morgan City are by private operators. Therefore, the database on vessel trips on the Atchafalaya River from Morgan City to GOM was examined as an option for the selection of port activity variables. As described earlier, the Atchafalaya River from Morgan City to the GOM is the main access channel providing the vital link for the delivery of offshore supply services. The database on non self-propelled vessel movements on this navigable waterway was selected to represent the port activity levels at Morgan City. As illustrated in Figure 4.1, self-propelled vessels account for 81 percent of the total vessel trips and are mainly recreational and commercial fishing vessels with no connection to OCS activities.

4.4.2. Historical Trends

The historical trends of the industry variables and the port activity variables are shown in Figure 4.2. The trends of OCS wells drilled and miles of pipeline approvals were discussed in an earlier section. The EP data, as expected, closely follow the number of exploratory wells. In the case of total vessel trips, the data points for 1997 and 1999 will remain as large outliers from the trend line. However, these wide variations did not affect the non self-propelled vessels category.

43

Table 4.7

Data and Analysis Variables

	Dev. Wells	Expl. Wells	Total Wells	Pipeline miles	EP	DOCD	Self-prop Vessel Trips	Non SP Vessel Trips	Total Vessel Trips
	(1)	(2)	(3)	(4)	(5)	(6)	(7)	(8)	(9)
1992	27	7	34	76	25	3	18,398	2,112	20,510
1993	29	12	41	52	25	4	21,540	2,225	23,765
1994	37	28	65	193	37	4	23,421	2,515	25,936
1995	51	34	85	139	38	8	25,302	2,805	28,107
1996	71	42	113	329	64	10	28,367	3,643	32,010
1997	88	84	172	285	105	11	30,168	4,371	34,539
1998	57	112	169	450	125	16	22,983	4,095	27,078
1999	49	123	172	512	168	14	15,479	3,127	18,606
2000	67	146	213	241	157	27	18,753	4,266	23,019
2001	60	148	208	711	150	37	--	--	---

Notes on data sources:
1. Columns 1 to 6 are from *Deepwater Gulf of Mexico 2002: America's Expanding Frontier* (MMS, 2002).
2. Columns 7 to 9 are from *Waterborne Commerce of the United States* (U.S. Army Corps of Engineers, 2000).

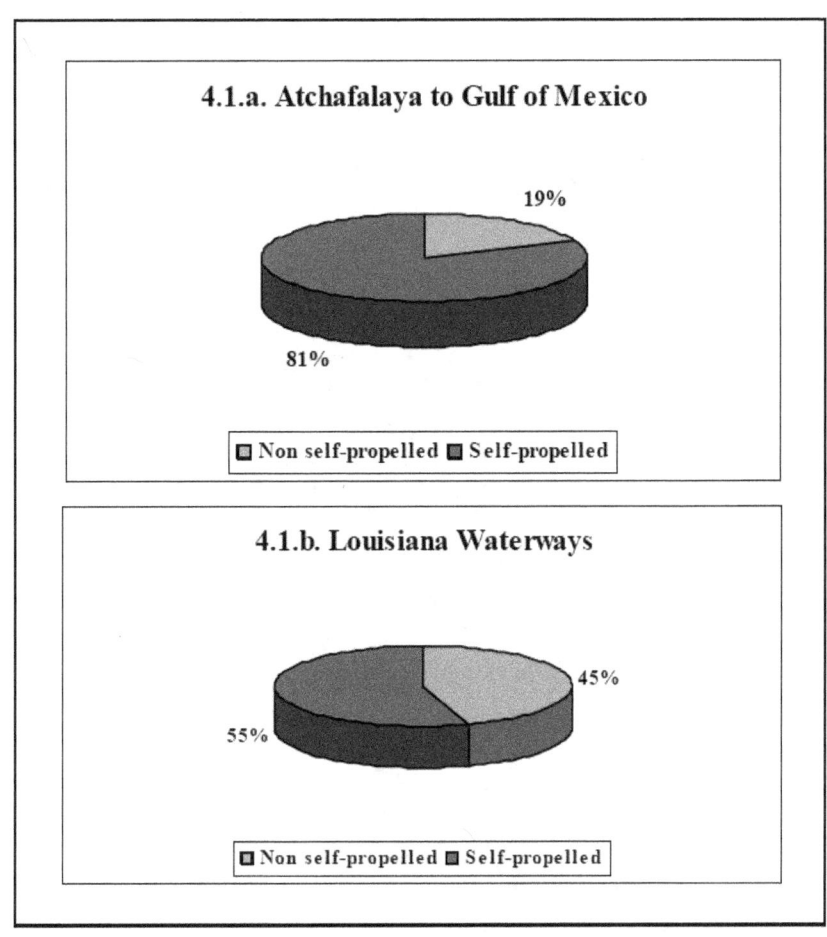

Figure 4.1.   Self-Propelled and Non Self-Propelled Vessel Trips on the
            Atchafalaya River from Morgan City to the Gulf of Mexico
            and on Other Louisiana Waterways.

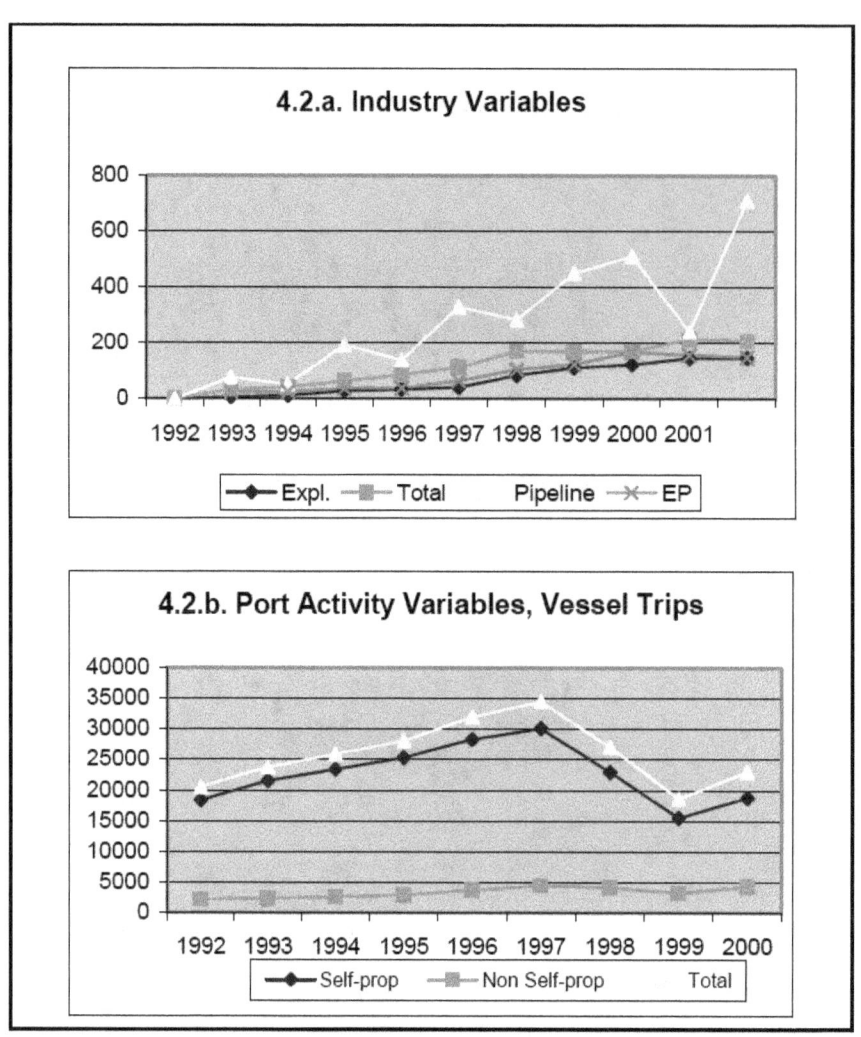

Figure 4.2. Variable Trends.

46

4.5. Estimating the Demand for Port Services

Six regression models were specified using each of the six industry variables as the independent variable and the number of non self-propelled vessels as the dependent variable. The model specifications and the complete computer output are included in Appendix B. A summary of model estimates is shown in Table 4.8.

Table 4.8

Regression Estimates for Vessel Traffic and Technical Relationships Between Variables

Independent Variable*	Model No.	Intercept	Regression Coefficient	R^2	F-Value
Number of development wells-drilled	4.1	1129.5 (3.02)	39.9 (6.0)	0.8371	35.97
Number of exploratory wells drilled	4.2	2364.0 (7.28)	13.40 (3.36)	0.6181	11.33
Total number of wells drilled	4.3	1796.0 (6.21)	12.21 (5.64)	0.8195	31.77
Miles of pipeline approved (lagged by one year)	4.4	2544.4 (5.72)	3.29 (2.21)**	0.4501	4.91
Number of EPs filed	4.5	2303.0 (5.87)	11.33 (2.85)	0.5375	8.13
Number of DOCDs filed	4.6	2248.5 (6.44)	92.0 (3.41)	0.6244	11.63

Notes: 1   * The dependent variable for all regressions is the number of non self-propelled vessel trips.
2.   Numbers in parentheses are t-values, and all t-values and F-values are significant at the 5% level
3.   ** Significant at the 10% level.

Variable Relationships Between OCS Wells Drilled and Vessel Traffic

The three models provided statistically significant and consistent estimates. The models with the total number and the number of development wells as the explanatory variable indicated very high R-square values.

The models were capable in explaining more than 80 percent of the variations in non self-propelled vessel traffic trips on the Atchafalaya River. Surprisingly, the development wells category that was dropped as a variable in the Port Fourchon analysis provided the "best fit" model in this case. The interpretation of the regression results could be expressed as that for every development well and exploratory well drilled in the OCS, the number of non self-propelled vessel trips will increase by 40 and 13 vessel trips respectively. The corresponding number for the total number of wells is 12 trips.

Pipeline Approvals and Vessel Traffic

The model where the miles of pipelines was the explanatory variable yielded statistically more significant results when the data lagged by one year was used in the model. This is in line with the observed phenomena where there is a gap between plan approvals and implementation.

47

4.6. Model Forecasts

The vessel trip forecasts were developed through 2010 for the Atchafalaya River from Morgan City to the GOM following similar procedures described earlier in this report. The six alternative forecasts made using the results of regression models and the forecasts of vessel trips derived from linear trend extrapolation are shown in Table 4.9.

While four of the forecasts deviate less than 10 percent of the extrapolated trend, two model forecasts are substantially lower than the trend. According to the trend extrapolation, the growth rate in vessel traffic will be about 5 percent a year; however, it is about 3 percent according to lower forecasts.

4.7. Structural Analysis and Policy Implications

Correlation Analysis

The correlation matrix in Table 4.10 provides a summary of the quantitative relationships for all variables included in this section. While columns 1 to 6 of the matrix are industry variables, columns 7 to 9 are port activity variables.

The relevant relationships between the dependent variable used in the regression analysis and other variables are indicated in column 8. High and positive correlation coefficients are observed between the number of non self-propelled vessels and the industry variables. The positive correlations confirm an a priory economic relationship that oil and gas industry expansion leads to higher port activity levels, leading to higher traffic levels. In contrast, the category of self-propelled vessels (column 7) representing mostly recreation vessels and commercial fishing vessels are negatively correlated with most of the industry variables.

In this section, we have examined the nature of OCS logistics services provided by the Morgan City supply base and the organizational structure in terms of public and private sector operations. The public port, which started as an operating port in the mid 1990's, remains as a potential service base that could expand operations in the future. The private sector operations that specialize in shipbuilding and repair services will continue to cater to a diversified market and have the capacity to accommodate the increasing demands of the expanding OCS oil and gas industry. Although the traffic volumes on the Atchafalaya River from Morgan City to the GOM will continue to grow, it is not likely to be a constraint for the expansion of port services.

Table 4.9

Model Forecasts of Vessel Traffic

Year	Model Number						Trend Extrapol.
	4.1	4.2	4.3	4.4	4.5	4.6	
	Independent Variable						
	Dev. Wells	Explor. Wells	Total Wells	Pipeline Miles	EP	DOCD	
(number of non self-propelled vessel trips)							
2000	4,266	4,266	4,266	4,266	4,266	4,266	4,266
2001	4,425	4,506	4,534	4,456	4,472	4,568	4,533
2002	4,584	4,746	4,801	4,646	4,679	4,870	4,801
2003	4,743	4,987	5,069	4,836	4,885	5,173	5,068
2004	4,902	5,227	5,336	5,025	5,092	5,475	5,336
2005	5,062	5,467	5,604	5,215	5,298	5,777	5,603
2006	5,221	5,707	5,872	5,405	5,504	6,079	5,871
2007	5,380	5,948	6,139	5,595	5,711	6,381	6,138
2008	5,539	6,188	6,407	5,785	5,917	6,684	6,406
2009	5,698	6,428	6,674	5,975	6,124	6,986	6,673
2010	5,857	6,668	6,942	6,165	6,330	7,288	6,941
Var. trend	3.99	17.93	21.92	57.71	18.22	3.28	N/A
Reg. Coeff.	39.90	13.40	12.21	3.29	11.33	92.00	N/A
Annual Growth	159.12	240.23	267.58	189.86	206.41	302.21	267.47
Variation from Trend							
	-1,084	-272	1	-776	-611	347	0

Table 4.10

Correlation Matrix for Analysis Variables – Morgan City

	Col. 1	Col. 2	Col. 3	Col. 4	Col. 5	Col. 6	Col. 7	Col. 8	Col. 9
Column 1	1.0000								
Column 2	0.5675	1.0000							
Column 3	0.7585	0.9670	1.0000						
Column 4	0.4932	0.7422	0.7400	1.0000					
Column 5	0.5408	0.9811	0.9438	0.8058	1.0000				
Column 6	0.5745	0.9250	0.9098	0.5271	0.8614	1.0000			
Column 7	0.5946	-0.2571	-0.0195	-0.0730	-0.3066	-0.2043	1.0000		
Column 8	0.9149	0.7862	0.9052	0.6155	0.7331	0.7902	0.3582	1.0000	
Column 9	0.7072	-0.1034	0.1369	0.0378	-0.1583	-0.0539	0.9871	0.5029	1.0000

Column 1 - Number of development wells drilled
Column 2 - Number of exploratory wells drilled
Column 3 - Total number of wells drilled
Column 4 - Miles of pipeline approvals
Column 5 - Number of exploration plans filed
Column 6 - Number of DOCD's filed
Column 7 - Number of self-propelled vessel trips
Column 8 - Number of none self-propelled vessel trips
Column 9 - Number of total vessel trips

5. Port of Iberia

The Port of Iberia is located in southcentral Louisiana along the Commercial Canal, approximately 7.5 mi north of the Gulf Intracoastal Waterway (GIWW), 9 mi north of Weeks Bay on the GOM, and 4.5 mi southwest of the city of New Iberia. The location and configuration of the Port of Iberia, a public port that specializes mainly in platform fabrication, repair, and maintenance, are strongly influenced by OCS supply activities. Maintaining direct and easy access routes to the GOM, improvements to the network of channels, slips, and land at the waterfront, and market promotion are high priorities for the Port.

The purpose of this analysis is to assess the Port of Iberia's role as a supply base to the OCS oil and gas industry and to examine the nature of supply adjustments made by the Port during the 1990's in response to the expansion of OCS activities. Since a comprehensive database is not available for the Port, the evaluation of adjustments is qualitative rather than quantitative. Quantitative analysis is performed, though, whenever data is available, i.e., for capital investment and port financial performance. A qualitative assessment of this nature is thought to be quite instructive and useful for public port infrastructure planning.

5.1. Port Location and Transportation Links

Access Channels

The access to the GOM is vital to the Port for delivery of large prefabricated structures and other offshore products. Several access channel options available to Port tenants and the major constraints of each are listed in Table 5.1.

1. *Commercial Canal/GIWW (East)/Atchafalaya Route.* Constraint: the 73 ft air-draft at the Highway 317 Bridge.
2. *Commercial Canal/GIWW/Acadiana Navigation Channel Route.* Constraint: the nine-foot depth of the Acadiana Navigation Channel. Because of environmental concerns (salt water intrusion and erosion), there are no plans to deepen this channel at present.
3. *Commercial Canal/GIWW (West)/Vermilion River Cutoff.* Constraint: the depth (8 ft) and width (80 ft) of the Vermillion River Cutoff. Feasibility studies conducted by the Port have identified this route, with the necessary modifications, as the best alternative for accessing the GOM. The project is currently awaiting Congressional approval for funding.
4. *Commercial Canal/GIWW (West)/Freshwater Bayou Canal Route.* Constraint: the longer distances and therefore time involved in using a bypass channel.

Table 5.1

Access Channels and Constraints

Channel	Location and Characteristics	Constraints
Commercial Canal	Port access channel 8 mi long Connects to GIWW, south	Actual Depth: 12 ft Actual Width: 25 ft
Gulf Intracoastal Waterway (GIWW)	8 mi south of port 140 mi west of Mississippi River 100 mi east of Calcasieu Ship Channel	Actual Depth: 12 ft Actual Width: 125 ft Authorized Depth: 16 ft Authorized Width: 50 ft
Atchafalaya River	30 mi east on GIWW	Actual Depth: 20 ft Actual Width: 200 ft Air draft: 73 ft at Hwy 317 bridge
Acadiana Navigation Channel	Extension of Commercial Canal to the south across Vermilion Bay	Actual Depth: 9 ft Actual Width: 200 ft
Vermilion River Cutoff	Northwest corner of Vermilion Bay	Authorized Depth: 8 ft Authorized Width: 80 ft
Freshwater Bayou Canal	25 mi southwest on GIWW	Authorized Depth: 12 ft Authorized Width: 125 ft Must pass through a lock: 12 ft deep x 84 ft wide

Source: *Master Development Plan* (Port of Iberia, 2000).

Highway Access

Two access roads running North-South connect the Port to Highway 90. Highway 90 is a four-lane highway, which is earmarked for improvements as a southern extension of Interstate 49 below Interstate 10. Average daily traffic counts (AADT) at two locations on Highway 90 indicate a volume to capacity (V/C) ratio of 70 percent, which is considered a good level of service (LOS) by transportation planners (Table 5.2). In addition, the Port is served by more than half a dozen Louisiana highways, which are fairly well maintained. According to the Louisiana Department of Transportation and Development, the current highway facilities are adequate and do not impose any constraints to Port operations.

Table 5.2

AADT Counts on Highway 90

Location	Number of Lanes	Volume (V)/ Capacity (C)	V/C Ratio	Level of Service (LOS)*
Hwy 90 North of Hwy 14	Four-lane	22,880/32,000	0.72	C
Hwy 90 near Hwy 329 junction	Four-lane	21,810/32,000	0.68	C

* The level of service is graded from A to F (where F is very congested).

Rail Access

Rail services to the port are provided by the BNSF, Union Pacific (UP), and the Louisiana Delta Railroad Company. BNSF and UP are mainline railroads providing an easterly route to New Orleans, a westerly route to Lake Charles and Houston, and northerly route to Opelousas. The Louisiana Delta Railroad Company, a short-line railroad company provides services between Vermillion and Iberia Parishes, and also operate spurs which service Avery Island and Weeks Island.

5.2. Port Infrastructure

5.2.1. Port Layout and Land Use

Businesses at the public sector of the Port of Iberia and several private sector businesses are engaged primarily in offshore metal fabrication activities. These activities are concentrated along Commercial Canal and Rodere Canal (Figure 5.1). The Port area which encompasses about 3,848 ac could be divided into four functional zones on the basis of ownership and major activities (Figure 5.2):

1. *Mixed Land Use (Zone 1)* - This area, approximately 1,475 ac located north of Port Road, is currently not accessible by water transportation. The land use is mixed with commercial, industrial, and residential uses. On a functional basis this area can be identified as the "service sector" of the Port, as most of its activities are oriented toward servicing Port needs. These range from technical and professional services to hotels and restaurants.
2. *Private Sector (Zone 2)* - This area, located to the west of Commercial Canal along Rodere Canal, is an industrial zone with a concentration of private sector operators. Most of the metal fabrication industries are located at nine slips on Rodere Canal, which provides waterway access to the GOM via Commercial Canal. Rodere Canal extends 6,400 ft in length, is 14 ft deep, and has bottom and top widths of 140 ft and 200 ft respectively. The southern section of this zone extends east of Commercial Canal, dividing the public Port property.

3. *Public Port (Zone 3)* - This area defines the public Port section. Public Port properties are located in two areas east of Commercial Canal, covering a total of 590 ac. In 1995, a 170 ac was added to the southern section. A detailed analysis of Port facilities is described below.
4. *Future Expansion (Zone 4)* - This area, 410 ac east of the public Port, is identified for future expansion.

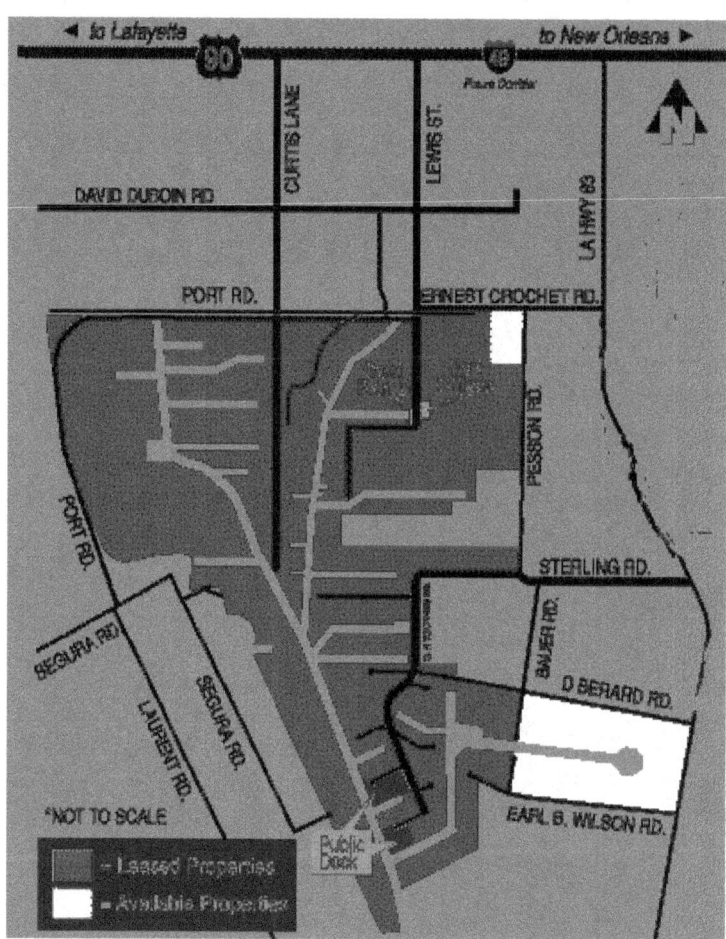

Figure 5.1. Port Layout and Plan Use.

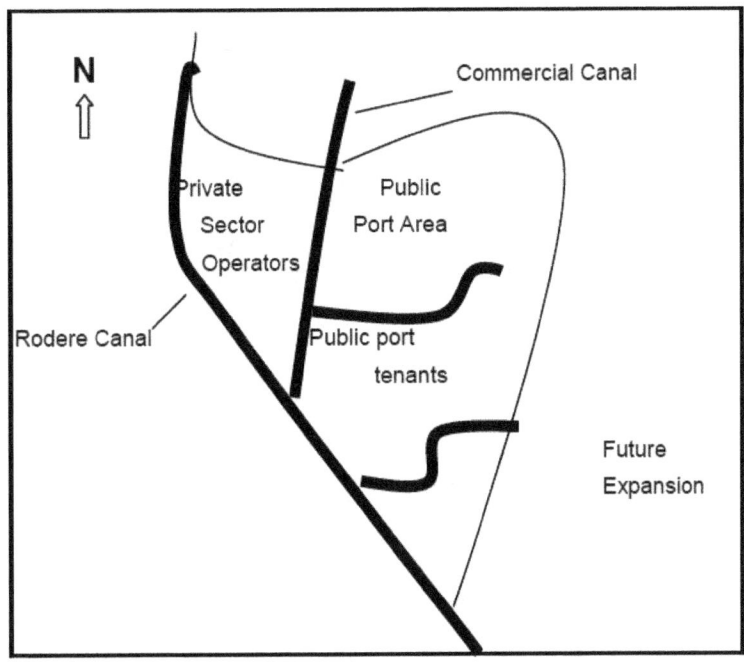

Figure 5.2. Functional Zones.

5.2.2. Public Port Organization and Operations

The Port of Iberia was created in 1938 by Act 128 of the Louisiana State Legislature and Act 486 in 1978. The Port's jurisdiction covers most of Iberia Parish and the communities of Jeanerette and Loreauville. The overall responsibility for the management of the public Port is entrusted to a seven-member Port Commission. The Commissioners, appointed by the parish government and the municipalities of Jeanerette and Loreauville, serve for a six-year term. An executive director is responsible for the management of Port operations. The general mission of the Port Commission is to cooperate with public and private organizations in promoting economic development, and creating employment opportunities by diversifying the local economy.

As a landlord port, the major activity of the public Port is to plan port facilities and lease them to the private sector tenants. An analysis of the lease information indicates that the Port has leased 279 ac of waterfront property to 47 tenants (Table 5.3). With 55 percent of the land leased beyond 2005, the Port is assured of a stable revenue stream for the next 10 to 15 years. A positive relationship also exists between the length of the lease term and the number of acres leased – leases extending beyond 2010 are about four times larger (with respect to the number of acres leased) than short-term leases.

Table 5.3

Analysis of Lease Operations

Lease Period	Number of Leases	Waterfront Acreage	Average Size (acres)	Percent of Total Leased Acreage
2000 - 2005	31	123.6	4.0	44
2006 - 2010	12	96.7	8.1	35
2011 - 2020	4	58.6	14.7	21
Total	47	278.9	5.9	100

Source: *Master Development Plan* (Port of Iberia, 2000).

Lease Rates

The lease rates charged by the Port depend on the location and the improvements made to the area in terms of land stabilization, buildings, access to bulkheads, etc. The main factors that determine lease rates are:

1. *Waterfront Location.* Lease rates for waterfront locations are about five times more than non-waterfront lands for similar sized areas. For example, less than one-acre waterfront sites are leased for approximately $6,500/ac/yr compared to non-waterfront lease rates of $1,300.
2. *Lease Site Size.* Lease rates are on a sliding scale with rates decreasing for larger lots. For example, 1999 lease rates per acre for waterfront sites less than one acre averaged $ 6,500 while sites larger than 20 ac averaged $1,800/ac.
3. *Cost of Site Improvements.* The current policy of the Port is to recover 6 percent of site improvement costs as annual rent.

5.2.3. Tenant Activities

The results of a survey[5] conducted in the Port area (including public Port and private sector firms around Commercial Canal and Rodere Canal) indicate that 71 percent of the businesses at the Port are in some form connected to the offshore supply industry (Table 5.4). Fabrication and repair services comprise the largest single activity with 29 percent while other offshore services make up 42 percent. However, this information is of limited value, as it includes a wide spectrum of industries from those engaged exclusively in offshore supply logistics (e.g., offshore supply boats) to those industries with very limited dependence (e.g., local retailers). Nevertheless it indicates that the local economic outlook is closely dependent on the offshore oil and gas industry.

---

[5] *Master Development Plan* (Port of Iberia, 2000).

Table 5.4

Classification of Businesses (1999)

Industry	Number of Business Units	Percent of the Sample
Offshore Supply Industries		
Fabrication	20	20
Repair Services	9	9
Other offshore services	43	42
Total Offshore	72	71
Other Industries	30	29
Grand Total	102	100

Fabrication Activities

The layout and major components of a typical fabrication yard is shown in Figure 5.3. It consists of three major components:

1. *Dock and Channel Slip.* The dock and slip area are used to assemble large structures as well as for loading and unloading.
2. *Fabrication Buildings.* The typical building configuration consists of several fabrication bays, equipped with overhead cranes, serving as work areas, material preparation areas, and equipment maintenance and storage areas.
3. *Yard Storage and Staging Area.* The yard staging area with concrete surface is usually used for cargo handling and as areas for equipment fabrication. The rest of the yard used for storage of raw materials is typically earthen surface stabilized with limestone.

5.2.4. Profile of a Port Tenant

Since data on private sector operations are scarce, a profile of a typical Port tenant was developed in order to gain some insights. The major characteristics of a typical business, such as the leasing terms for public facilities, site improvements made by the operator, the products and services provided, the total payroll, etc., are provided in Table 5.5. Similarly, Table 5.6 was developed to show the typical procedures adopted when expanding Port facilities with public and private sector participation.

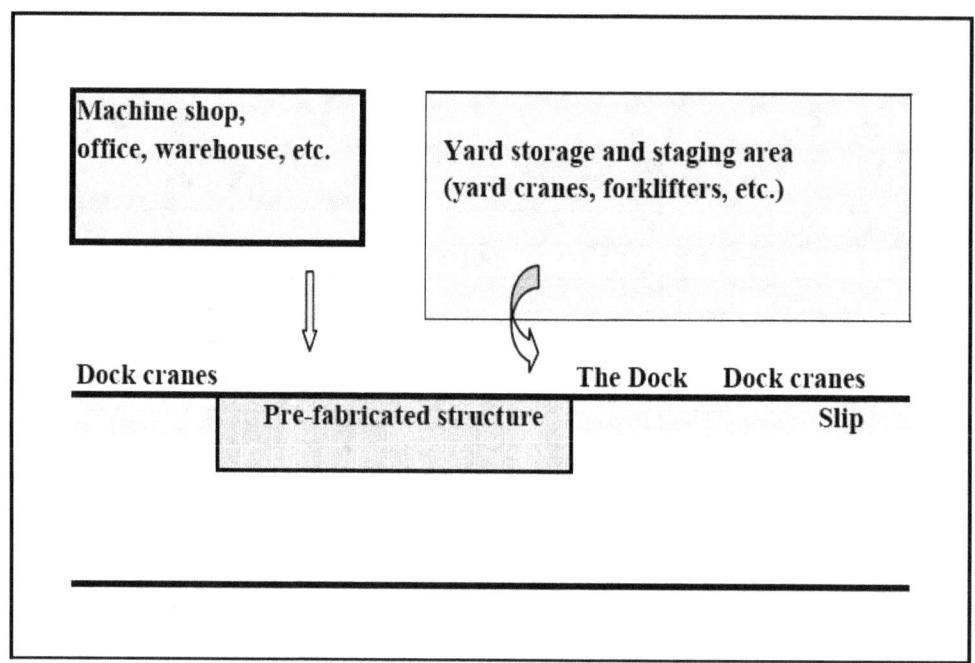

Figure 5.3. Layout of a Typical Prefabrication Terminal.

Table 5.5

Profile of a Tenant

Company
The ABC Company (ABC) is a tenant at the Port of Iberia. It has been engaged in metal fabrication since 1995. For the past five years ABC has manufactured process systems and equipment, including cold boxes, thermal vacuum control systems, and custom-engineered cryogenic and vacuum systems. Major customers include Beltech, Air Liquide, Praxair, Messar, Lockheed-Martin, Philips Petroleum, NASA, and other government-private sector joint ventures.

Annual Tonnage - The ABC Company assembles 25 units per year. Each unit averages 255,000 pounds. Average annual tonnage is estimated at 3,200 tons.

Employment – The ABC Company employs approximately 100 people and 20 contract welders, with an annual payroll of about $2.5 million.

Lease Agreement
Primary term and rental - The initial lease is for a ten-year period (1995-2005) at an annual rent of $140,400, with an option to renew for three more 10-year periods by mutual consent.

Location and access - The 20-ac site, leased from the Port, has 1,300 linear ft of water frontage with a 100-ft bulkhead. The site is well connected to the regional highway system, and the raw material supply by trucks is satisfactory.

Buildings and other improvements - In addition to the slip and the 100-ft bulkhead, the present improvements at the site consist of (1) a stabilized fabrication and lay-down yard, (2) an open, concrete slab (100'x200') yard used for fabrication work, (3) a 55,000 ft^2 fabrication building, and (4) a smaller fabrication building (15,000 ft^2 capacity). The 55,000 ft^2 fabrication building consists of three 50'x225' fabrication bays: one bay for small fabrication; one for pipe spooling and material preparation; and the third for equipment storage and warehouse space. The 15,000 ft^2 building consists of one fabrication bay of 35'x150' and two 32'x150' material preparation bays.

Future Plans
The ABC Company plans to expand activities at the site by adding another fabrication building.

Table 5.6

Fabrication Building: A New Project

Project Description
The ABC Company plans to construct a 27,500 ft^2 fabrication building in order to meet the increasing demand for fabricated materials. The new building will provide two 75'x150' fabrication bays and one 50'x100' warehouse bay. Each bay will be equipped with electrical and mechanical welding stations and two 20 ton double girder overhead bridge cranes.

Tenant's Equipment
The ABC Company is committed to supplying welding machines and equipment, plasma torches, and fitting equipment, estimated at $250,000.

Project Cost and Modes of Financing
The estimated project cost is $1.65 million. The Port of Iberia Port Commission applied to the Louisiana Port Construction and Development Priority Program (PCDP) for funding for the project. The PCPD will fund $1.25 million of the project with the Port providing the remaining $400,000.

Port Revenue from the Project
The ABC Company is committed to paying the Port an additional $98,000 in rent/yr for the additional improvements.

Other Project Benefits
Tonnage - The ABC Company estimates that total output will increase by 50 percent. The new facility will increase output by 1,600 tons enlarging total output to 4,800 tons.

Employment and payroll - The project is estimated to generate 52 jobs with an annual payroll of $1.2 million.

5.3. Historical Trends

5.3.1. Port Capital Investments

In the 1990's the Port of Iberia embarked on a systematic program to improve and expand Port facilities with state funds, federal grants, and self generated revenues. The PCDP program funded most of the development projects. The historical cumulative trend of these investments is illustrated in Figure 5.4. Projects undertaken during the 1992-2000 period can be classified into three functional categories and roughly corresponds with three time periods:

1. *Projects to provide basic port infrastructure and amenities in the early 1990's.*
   The development of a wastewater collection system, sanitary sewer collection, and a drinkable water system were undertaken during this period providing the

basic amenities at the Port. In addition, the public dock area was developed, expanding the basic infrastructure available for public use. By making these investments in the early 1990's, the Port laid the foundation for growth.

2. *Port expansion projects in the mid 1990's.* A major expansion of the Port was undertaken in 1995 by purchasing additional land and by developing a new 170-ac slip. This project provided the Port with opportunities to expand its customer base.

3. *Port expansion projects in the late 1990's.* During this period, the Port made terminal improvements such as building bulkheads, warehouses, etc., sharing the costs with tenants. All tenants who participated in these projects were engaged in offshore supply activities, indicating the demand pressures for Port services.

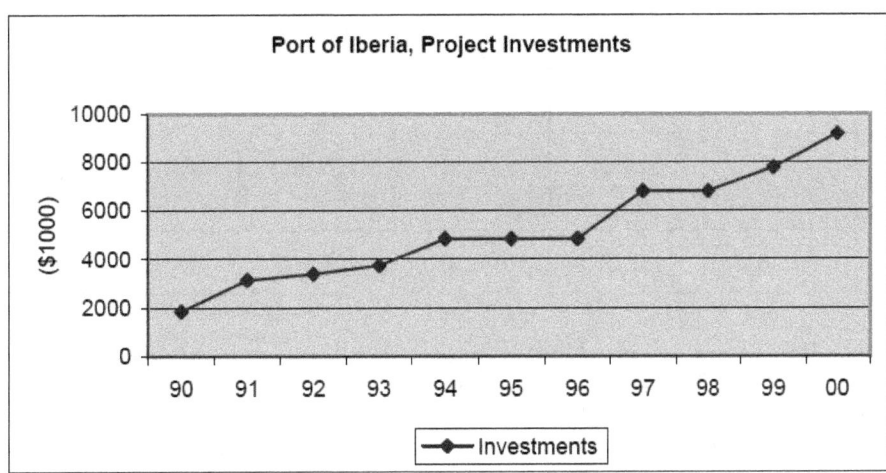

Figure 5.4. Capital Expenditures, Cumulative Trend (1990-2000).

5.3.2. Port Financial Performance

Table 5.7 shows the Port's financial performance during the 1990's from annual financial reports.

Growth Trends in Total Assets and Operating Revenues
During the 1992-2000 period, total assets at the Port grew by 125 percent, while operating revenues grew by 205 percent (Figure 5.5a). This indicates better returns on assets, which in turn, points to the increased demand for facilities.

Table 5.7

Financial Performance Trends, Selected Years

	1992 ($)	1994 ($)	1996 ($)	1998 ($)	2000 ($)	Change 1992 - 2000 (%)
Operating Revenue	455,429	744,445	1,021,856	1,085,665	1,388,130	205
Operating Expenses	411,105	604,965	438,612	578,043	554,976	35
Depreciation	161,496	356,701	358,109	690,593	813,940	404
Non-operating Income	128,577	61,684	119,227	125,007	187,628	46
Net Income	11,405	-155,537	344,362	-57,964	206,842	1,714
Total Assets	14,931,158	17,491,571	28,599,228	30,356,119	33,610,795	125

Source: Annual Financial Reports, Port of Iberia.

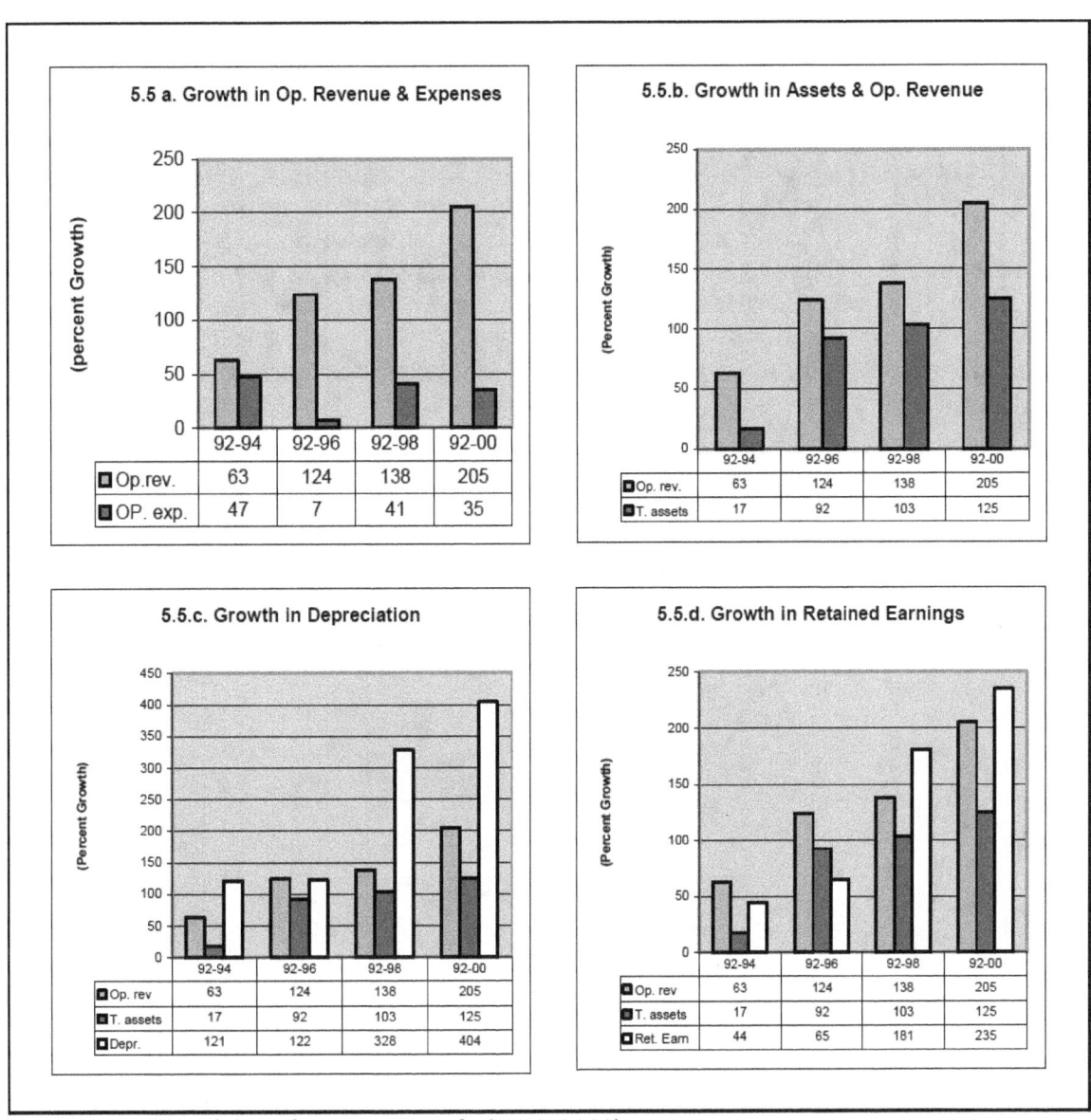

Figure 5.5. Financial Performance Trends (1992-2000).

The growth rate for operating revenues and expenses were 205 percent and 35 percent respectively (Figure 5.5b). This is typical for a landlord port with expenses that are substantial in the initial stages (i.e., salaries, insurance, marketing, and promotion) and then more or less constant thereafter.

Growth Trends in Depreciation

Depreciation grew by 404 percent during the 1992-2000 period, a rate faster than most other indexes (Figure 5.5c). The reason for this growth is the aggressive capital investment program initiated by the Port. Since depreciation is a noncash accounting expense, is available to the Port for reinvestment or to meet any other Port expenses.

Growth in Retained Earnings

With steep increases in depreciation and increases in net income, the retained earnings of the Port increased by 245 percent during the analysis period (Figure 5.5d).

Sources and Uses of Funds

Major sources of operating revenues and expenses for the Port are shown in Figure 5.6. Eighty-seven percent of the operating revenues are derived from leasing Port facilities. Each year the Port tries to recover 6 percent of its capital costs (for site improvements) from its leaseholders. According to the terms of the lease agreement, routine maintenance of leased facilities is the responsibility of tenants. The revenues from contract and dockage fees are primarily from public dock operations performed by private labor contractors.

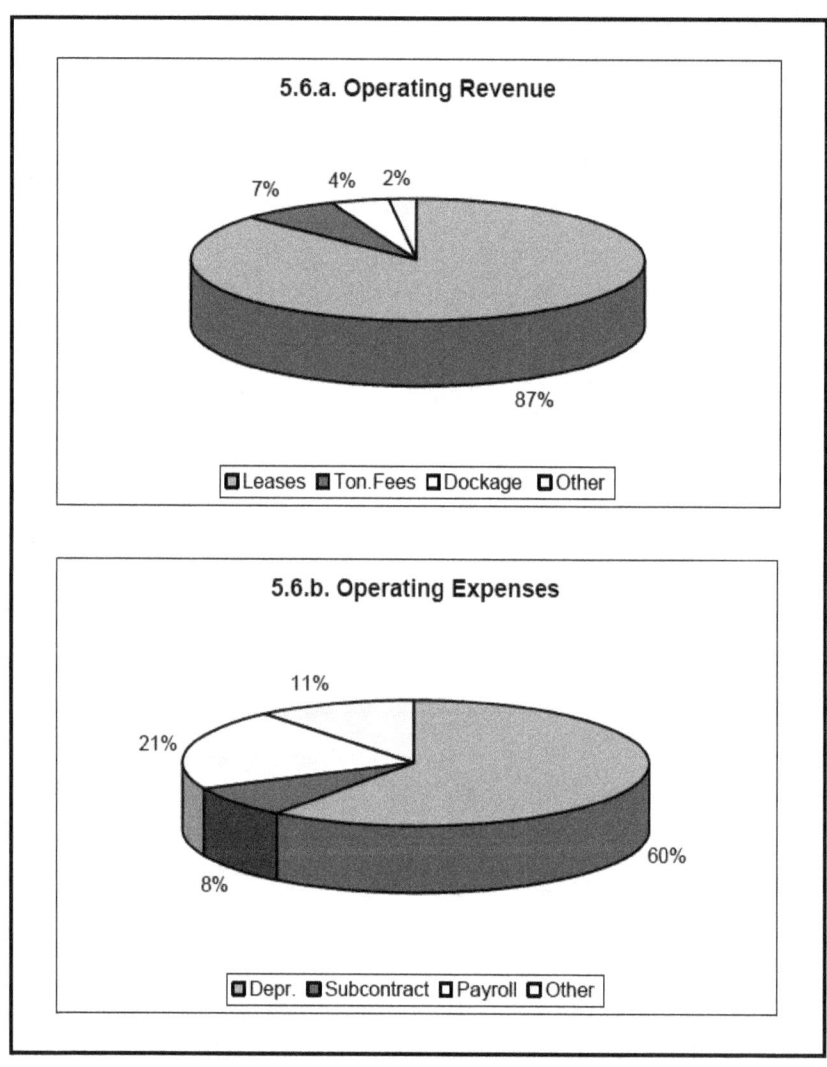

Figure 5.6. Financial Indicators, Sources, and Uses of Funds (2000).

5.3.3. Port Employment

Results from a survey on Port employment data are shown in Table 5.8. The survey, conducted in 1999, was completed for the Port's Master Plan Study. The results are a compilation of a mail survey and personal interviews. According to survey estimates, 3,538 persons were employed in Port-related activities in 1999 generating an annual payroll of $118 million by the public Port and the private sector Port tenants around the Commercial Canal area. Although the vast majority of these workers were engaged in the offshore oil and gas service sector, it is difficult to desegregate them because of the interrelated nature of activities.

Table 5.8

Employment by Job Categories

Job Category	Occupations Included	Number Employed
Administrative/Professional	Managers, engineers, foremen, supervisors	606
Technicians	Electronic and engineering technicians	164
Sales/Clerical/Support Services	Shipping, dispatchers, clerical, security, maintenance workers, etc	337
Skilled Labor	Electricians, welders, divers, fitters, etc	1,069
Transportation and Equipment Pperators	Crane/truck/heavy equipment operators	232
Mariners	Boat captains, mates, and seamen	380
Laborers/Helpers	Painters, riggers, warehousemen, shop hand	750
Total		3,538

Source: Port of Iberia, Master Development Plan, 2000

5.4. Conclusions

Constraints imposed by the existing access channel from the port to the GOM are a major limitation in expanding OCS services from the port. Currently, the port is sponsoring a project to develop an access channel 20 feet in depth and 125 feet wide with the U.S. Army Corps of Engineers. The route selected consists of the Commercial Canal, a section on the GIWW to the west and then to gain access to the GOM through Freshwater Bayou. The total distance of this option is 51 miles including the distance from the mouth of the Freshwater Bayou to the 20-foot contour of the GOM[6].

---

[6] Benefit-Cost Analysis for Acadiana Gulf of Mexico Access Channel, Coastal Engineering and Environmental Consultants, Inc., July 2001

The location of the port with its connections to highways and rail, the availability of trained and skilled labor, the proximity to GOM, and healthy financial position of the port lay down a strong foundation for future development. The development of port infrastructure which started in the late 1990's continues expanding the capabilities of the Port. Recently the Port expanded its capacity by adding new waterfront land and extending the network of channels and slips. The port's marketing activities and financial performance are good indicators of the offshore industry's demand for port services since more than 60 percent of the Port's activities are oil and gas industry-related. With 55 percent of Port lands under long-term lease (beyond 2005), the Port is assured of a stable source of revenue over the next decade. Although operating revenues tripled over the 1992-2000 period and operating expenses grew at a much slower rate, net income at the Port was inconsistent. This was due to the substantial increase in depreciation of added assets.

6. Port of Galveston

The Port of Galveston is located on Galveston Bay 9.3 mi inland from the GOM. The public Port, as presently constituted, was created in 1940 by City Charter, and remains a political subdivision of the City of Galveston. The Port is managed by a 7-member board consisting of one City Council representative and six members appointed by the City Council. Two members are appointed each year resulting in staggered terms while all appointments are for three years. The stated mission of the Port is to manage its assets and resources so as to create optimum economic benefit to the local community. The analysis in this chapter examines the trends of growth in OCS activities at the port during the 1990's which coincides with the period of expansion in OCS oil and gas activities.

6.1. Port Location and Transportation Links

Channel Access

Public port facilities are strategically located, providing easy access to the GOM and the inland waterways network. The Galveston Ship Channel serves as the main access channel to the port. It is maintained at a minimum depth of 40 ft and a minimum width of 1,200 ft. Sailing time from open sea to the public docks, located 9.3 mi on the Ship Channel, is estimated at 30 minutes. The Port's location on the GIWW which connects with the Mississippi River system provides access to barge transportation.

A classification of vessel traffic on the Galveston Ship Channel analyzed by types of vessels, by domestic or foreign, and by draft is shown in Table 6.1. Ninety-three percent of the vessel fleet using the channel is by vessels with less than 18-foot draft and mainly for domestic services. The tanker traffic accounted for 14 percent of the traffic volumes.

Table 6.1

Analysis of Vessel Traffic on Galveston Ship Channel, 2001

Vessel Draft	Passenger/Dry Cargo	Tanker	Tow or Tug	Total
Foreign				
18 ft and less	846	4	1	851
> 18 feet	329	52	0	381
Total-Foreign	1,175	56	1	1,232
Domestic				
18 ft and less	11,884	2,272	4,273	18,429
> 18 feet	2	568	2	572
Total-Domestic	11,886	2,840	4,275	19,001
Total	13,061	2,896	4,276	20,233

Highways

Highway 45 is the main access to the Port. It connects to Interstate 10 and other major roads in Houston which is 49 mi from Galveston.

Railroads

The Galveston Railroad, L.C. (GVSR), a short-line railroad company, operates rail services at the Port. The company operates 43.3 mi of tract and with connections to BNSF and UP. The rail infrastructure is owned by the City of Galveston and has been leased to the present operator (GVSR) since 1987.

6.2. Port Infrastructure

The cargo throughput from all terminals at the Port of Galveston exceeded 4.2 million tons in 2001 with 76 percent of the total consisting of bulk cargos and the rest as containers and general cargo (Table 6.2). The Port with 300 acres of waterfront land on Galveston Island and 549 acres on Pelican Island included 10 mid-stream berths and 20 alongside berths with more than one million square feet of warehouse space and on-dock rail services. Terminals at the Port can be broadly classified on a functional basis into four major categories: container and break-bulk cargo, bulk cargo, industrial, and cruise ship (Table 6.3).

Table 6.2

Port Tonnage (2001)

Bulk Cargo		Container and Other	
Cargo Type	Tonnage	Cargo Type	Tonnage
Grain	2,365,904	Container	732,572
Sugar	372,670	RO/RO	97,834
Cement	193,607	General	21,439
Liquid-bulk	297,715	Bananas/Fruit	188,993
Total	3,229,896	Total	1,040,838
Total (%)	76	Total (%)	24

Source: Port of Galveston

6.2.1. Container and Break-bulk Cargo Terminals

Four terminals are included in this category: one container terminal, two roll-on/roll-off (RO/RO) terminals, and a terminal handling fresh fruit. The container terminal, which is managed by the Port of Houston, consists of a two berth dock 1,350 ft in length with a 40 ft water depth. Several mutually beneficial economic factors form the background for this collaborative arrangement between two independent public port authorities. The terminal at Galveston was a convenient outpost for the Port of Houston to divert traffic from the congested Houston Ship Channel. Further, the Port of Houston intended to use its business contacts and marketing information to attract more shippers and shipping lines to the new terminal managed

Table 6.3

Classification of Cargo Terminals

Terminal	Operator	Type of Activity
Container and Break-bulk Cargo Terminals		
Pier 10	Port of Houston	Container
Pier 16/18	Del Monte Fresh Produce	Bananas and other fresh fruit
Pier 34	"K" Line	RO/RO – vehicle handling
Pier 37	Wallenius Wilhelmsen Lines	RO/RO – vehicle handling
Bulk Cargo Terminals		
Pier 30/32	ADM/Farmland Industries Inc.	Grain elevator
Pier 35/36	Imperial Sugar Company	Sugar
Pier 28		Cement
Industrial Terminals		
Pier 14	Smith-Hamm, Inc.	Vessel repair and fabrication
Pier 34	Cooper Cameron Corp., Deep Flex Division	Manufacture flexible pipes
Pelican Island	Newpark Shipbuilding-Pelican Island, Inc.	Vessel repair and fabrication
Pelican Island	Edison Chouest Offshore, C Port Galveston LP	Offshore multi-service (planned)
Cruise Ship and Other Services		
Pier 19-22	Port of Galveston	Tourism
Pier 25	Carnival Cruise Lines Royal Caribbean International	Cruise ships
Pelican Island	Galveston Terminals	Bunker fuel for vessels
Pier 19	Port of Galveston	Commercial fishing

by them. For the Port of Galveston, it was an opportunity to lease an underutilized terminal and collaborate with a port partner with larger assets in terms of financial resources and management know-how. In 2001, the terminal handled 732,572 tons of cargo, an increase of approximately 4 percent over 2000 tonnage. The Port of Houston is presently attempting to attract a new operator at the terminal since the current operator ceased operations in June 2002. In the meantime, the Port of Houston continues to pay their lease payments to the Port of Galveston.

The two RO/RO terminals mainly handle farm vehicles and construction equipment (Table 6.2 and Figure 6.1). Cargo transfer at RO/RO terminals is by driving in or driving out cargo using trailers in and out of the vessel. In the case of farm vehicles, the vehicles are driven out of the vessel over a ramp for unloading. Other cargo, such as construction equipment may be in containers already loaded on to trailers or stacked without trailers. In the latter case a tractor trailer will move into the ships hold, load the containers on board by fork-loaders and driven out.

The two terminals also handle other break-bulk cargos: forest products (lumber, linerboard, plywood, newsprint, waste paper, pulp, and paper) and cotton bales. These are handled by conventional methods either using ship's gear or using shore cranes. The cargo delivery could either be direct delivery, in which case cargo is transferred direct to rail, barge, or trucks for inland transportation or will be stored in port warehouses for delivery later to consignees.

The fresh fruit terminal is managed by Del Monte Inc. and imports bananas from Guatemala and exports paper and plantation supplies. Major facilities at the terminal include a two-berth dock (1,200 ft in length with a 34 ft water depth) and 65,000 ft^2 of refrigerated warehouse space.

6.2.2. Bulk Cargo Terminals

The bulk cargo terminals consist of a grain export elevator operated by Archer Daniels Midland/Farmland Industries, a sugar terminal, and a bulk cement terminal that began operating in December 1998. The cement silo complex located at Pier 28 is designed to ship about 2,800 tons/day of imported cement by truck and rail out of the port. Rail service to the bulk terminals is provided by GVSR, and handles about 50,000 carloads/yr.

6.2.3. Industrial Terminals

Four industrial terminals are engaged in offshore activities. A detailed analysis of these terminals is presented below in Section 6.3.

6.2.4. Cruise Ship Terminals

The cruise ship industry is the fastest growing activity at the Port. In September 2000, renovations to the Texas Cruise Ship Terminal on Galveston Island were completed at a cost of $10.6 million. This is the greatest one time investment in improvements to a single facility in the Port's 175-year history. Terminal facilities, located at Piers 23 through 26, consist of a 49,600 ft^2 embarkation area, a 60,800 ft^2 disembarkation area, and a 137,800 ft^2 cruise terminal area. Royal Caribbean International Lines and Carnival Cruise Lines operate this terminal. The enlarged terminal combining piers 23-26 is referred to as Pier 25.

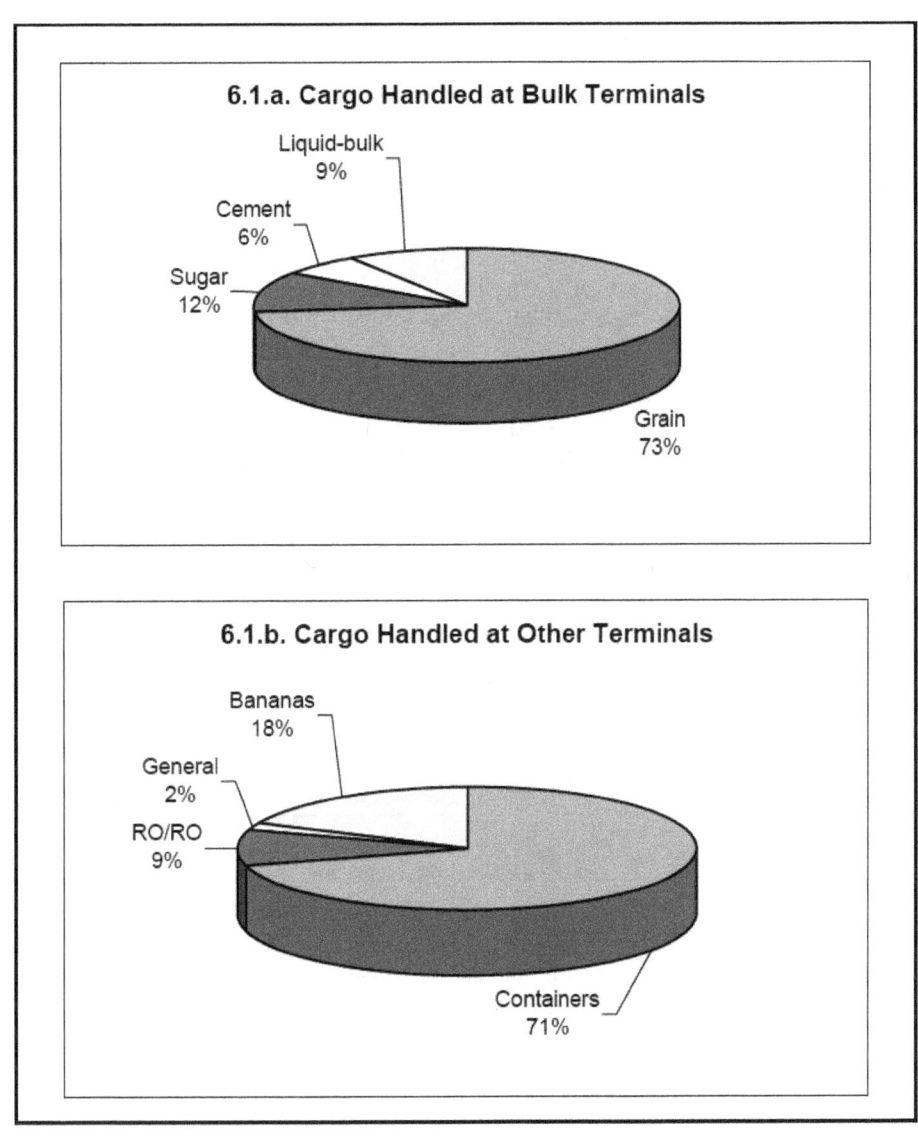

Figure 6.1. Tonnage by Major Categories (2001).

6.3. Offshore Supply Activities and Major Operators

6.3.1. Smith-Hamm, Inc.

At Pier 14's Marine Repair Facility, Smith-Hamm, Inc. is engaged in repair and maintenance of vessels and offshore rigs. Infrastructure facilities include a 1,500-ft dock, with a minimum water depth of 24 ft, and a 35,000 ft^2 staging area. In 1999, the company expanded its operations at the Port by leasing an additional six acres of waterfront land. Smith-Hamm typically employs 100-125 people, depending on project requirements, and maintains a 3.5-ac offshore repair facility on the Houston Ship Channel.

6.3.2. Cooper Cameron Corp-Deep Flex Division

In March 1999 the Port signed a five-year lease agreement with Cooper Cameron Corp-Deep Flex Division for Pier 34's Manufacturing Facility. The terminal, with a water depth of 40 ft and 44,500 ft^2 of covered space, is the main facility supporting Deep Flex operation. The firm specializes in the manufacture of flexible pipes for the offshore oil and gas industry and is expected to construct a $20 million portable conveyor system that connects the manufacturing facility to the loading vessel. Deep Flex estimates two vessel calls a month and has identified offshore drilling sites in the GOM, South America, West Africa, and Eastern Canada as potential markets for their product. Table 6.4 describes Deep Flex's planned operations at the Port.

6.3.3. First Wave/Newpark Shipbuilding-Pelican Island, Inc.

First Wave/Newpark Shipbuilding-Pelican Island, Inc. operates a 110-ac vessel repair and maintenance facility at the Pelican Island Marine Repair Facility. The company operates a network of five yards offering repair and maintenance services, environmental services, and new construction. Table 6.5 describes Newpark's operations at the Port.

Table 6.4

Cooper Cameron Corp-Deep Flex Division Planned Development

Development Stage/Facilities	Description
Lease Agreement	Signed March 1999 for a 5-yr term
Port Facilities	44,500 ft^2 covered terminal at Pier 34
Planned Construction	Construction of a portable conveyor system $20 million estimated investment
Manufacturing Schedule	Year 1 - 10.5 km of flexible pipe Year 2 - 50 km Year 3 - 150 km/yr thereafter
Shipping	Year 1 - 2 ship/month by specialized vessels laying pipes
Employment	Year 1 - 25 employees Year 3 - 150 employees

6.3.4. Edison Chouest Offshore/C Port Galveston, LP

In April 2000, the Port entered into a lease agreement with Edison Chouest Offshore, C Port Galveston, LP (Chouest) for the development of an offshore multi-service terminal. The 100-ac site, located on port land on Pelican Island, is an indication of the increase in demand for offshore services in the WPA. Chouest plans to develop a multi-service facility known as C Port Galveston Full Service Center. Upon completion, the facility will create a centralized hub for goods and services required for deepwater offshore operations in the WPA. C Port Galveston will transport offshore fuel, water, cement, and liquid mud in bulk form, and various machinery and equipment mostly carried as deck cargo. Table 6.6 describes Chouest's operations at the Port.

The planned developments Cooper Cameron Corp and by Edison Chouest Offshore is behind schedule, and their business plans seem to be on hold.

Table 6.5

Newpark Shipbuilding, Pelican Island, Inc., Profile of a Marine Repair Facility

Major Characteristics	Description

Location	110-ac facility at Pelican Island, Port of Galveston
	Operates 4 other yards:
	    2 on the Houston Ship Channel
	    2 in the Galveston area

Facilities	Multi-plant firm 5,000-ton dry dock, water depths up to 40 ft Covered slip served by 500-ton crane capacity 280,000 ft^2 of covered space for various activities
Services - Repairs	Repairs, conversions, and modifications to inland and ocean barges Top-side and in-water repairs to vessels OSV stretch jobs Converting offshore rigs Double-skinning of barges
Services - New Construction	Complementary capabilities at different yards make them mutually supporting in new construction
Services - Fabrication	Fabrication of offshore equipment Construction of oil platforms
Services - Environmental	Barge cleaning Wastewater treatment from vessels and rigs Gas-free services Marine chemist services

Table 6.6

Edison Chouest Offshore Service Center, Major Stages of Planned Development

Development Stage/Facilities	Description

Lease Conditions	Signed in April 2000 for a primary term of 10 yr
	Port revenue:
	    Year 1 - $100,000
	    Year 2 - $170,000
	    Year 3 - $325,000/yr thereafter

Facility Development (3 Phases)	Phase One: Engineering, site work, marketing, and promotion Phase Two: Construction Phase Three: Plant operation
Facilities and Cost	2,100 linear ft of water frontage and land area of 100 ac $89 million investment
Products and Services	One-stop service center for goods and services required in offshore deepwater drilling operations
Projected Employment	250-300 jobs will be created in operational phase

6.4. Development Trends

The infrastructure facilities at Port of Galveston have steadily increased during the last three decades. The port-owned waterfront land, for example, increased from about 299 ac in 1965 to 850 ac in 2000, almost tripling the size of the Port (Figure 6.2). The fastest growing port sectors in the 1990's were the cruise ship industry and OCS service activities. The development trends of OCS activities at the Port clearly indicate the adjustments made by the offshore service providers. Out of the four port tenants presently engaged in OCS activities, three moved to the port in the 1990's and the other tenant expanded activities during this time period. A summary of major developments:

- The operator at the Marine Repair Facility in Pier 14, Smith-Hamm, Inc., expanded operations by leasing an additional six acres of port land in 1998,
- The Manufacturing Facility at Pier 34, operated by Cooper Cameron Corp-Deep Flex Division, leased port land and started operations in 1999,
- The Pelican Island Marine Repair Facility operated by Newpark Shipbuilding-Pelican Island Inc., leased a 110-ac facility in 1997, and
- Edison Chouest began construction of C Port Galveston in 2000.

As a result of the above developments, port tenants serving the offshore industry increased their share of leased port-owned land to 27 percent in 2000 from 4 percent in 1993 (Figure 6.3).

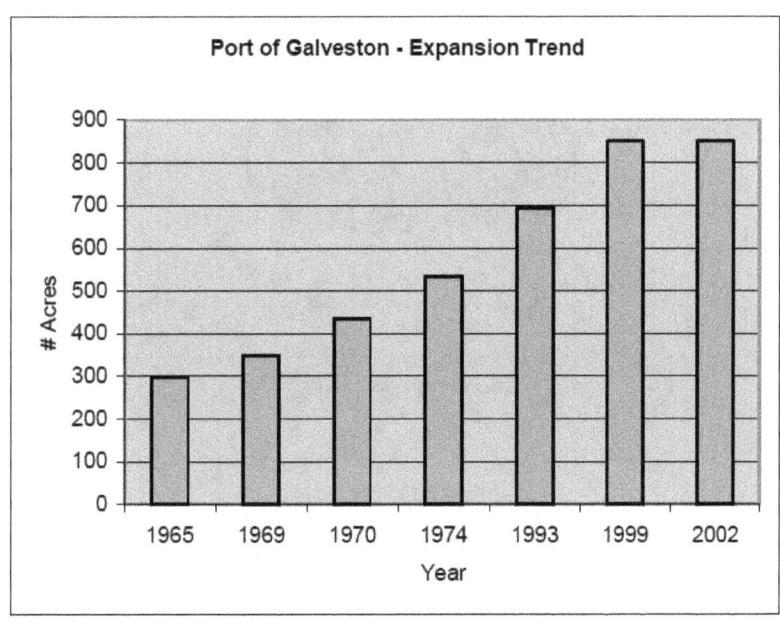

Figure 6.2. Port Owned Waterfront Land.

6.4.1. Structural Changes in the Industry

Although the industry-wide expansion in offshore activities was emphasized in this report, the regional differentials in expansion patterns were not evaluated. With most of the offshore expansion projects on hold in the Port of Galveston, a brief analysis of macroeconomic variables was undertaken to examine regional trends.

6.4.2. Analysis of Industry Trends in Louisiana and Texas

To start with, the numbers employed in the oil and gas industry and the state personal income from 1992 to 2000 for Texas and Louisiana were selected for a trend analysis. The data observations and the analysis results are shown in Table 6.7. The data indicate that the oil and gas sector in Texas is about five times larger (288,003/55917 = 5.15) than that of Louisiana in terms of the number employed in 1992. In contrast, in 2000 it is (216,260/55,086=3.93) only about four-times larger. However, this result has two major weaknesses in determining long-term changes in the industry. First, as they are point estimates, a peak or a valley in data in one year can skew the results. Second, for a comparative analysis to be valid, the economic conditions in both regions have to be stable during the period.

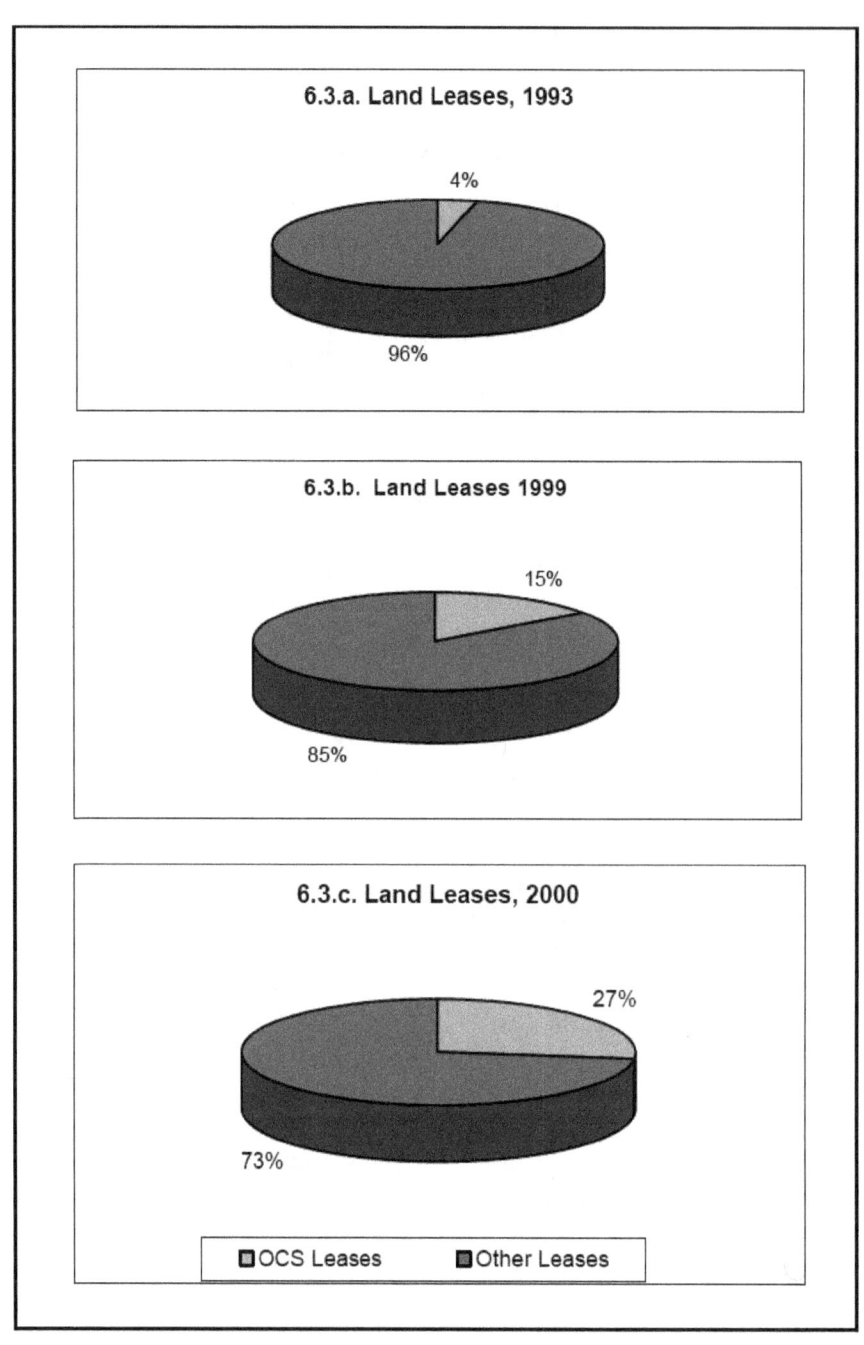

Figure 6.3. Land Leased to OCS Industries (1993, 1999, and 2000).

Table 6.7

Analysis of Long-Term Trends in the Oil and Gas Industry for
Louisiana and Texas, 1992-2000

Year	State Personal Income (Million $)		Employment in Oil and Gas Industry (1,000 jobs)	
	Texas	Louisiana	Texas	Louisiana
Data				
1992	337,934	72,466	288,003	55,917
1993	356,784	75,911	278,841	54,970
1994	377,583	80,871	272,372	56,469
1995	402,097	84,573	245,029	54,824
1996	428,726	87,879	226,052	56,210
1997	468,950	92,286	240,872	61,458
1998	511,964	97,458	238,944	64,473
1999	539,527	99,052	219,844	54,573
2000	586,587	103,630	216,260	55,086
Trend Analysis Results				
Trend1992-2000	7,200	4,500	-3,600	300
Forecast 2010	--	--	122,530	61,339

Source: U.S. Bureau of Labor Statistics (Website: http//www.bls.gov.).

Trend Analysis

A trend analysis, that estimates the trend-line minimizing squared deviations for all observations are shown under trend analysis in Table 6.7. State personal income in Texas increased by $7.2 million a year during the period compared to $4.5 million in Louisiana. From a qualitative analysis since both states experienced steady growth, the patterns of growth are comparable. In terms of numbers employed in the oil and gas industry, Texas on the average lost 3,600 jobs/yr compared to 300 jobs/yr gain in Louisiana. Based on this analysis, there is evidence to indicate that structural changes are taking place in the oil and gas industry – moving activities to Louisiana. A rigorous analysis is beyond the purview of this report. Assuming these trends to continue, the numbers employed in Texas in 2010 will be about twice that of Louisiana.

6.4.3. Port of Galveston and Industry Trends

Another added reason for the slow progress in offshore oil and gas projects at the Port of Galveston may be the timing of the investments. In order to examine this hypothesis the same data described earlier in Table 6.7 were arranged as three year moving averages and the percentage change for the periods were calculated (Table 6.8). Results indicate that both Texas and Louisiana experienced severe downturns in the industry during the 1997-2000-period. In fact, when the effects of both states are combined it is the most severe downturn in a decade.

Table 6.8

Analysis of Long-Term Trends in the Oil and Gas Industry for
Louisiana and Texas, Three Year Moving Averages, 1992-2000

Year	State Personal Income (Million $)		Employment in Oil and Gas Industry (1,000 jobs)	
	Texas	Louisiana	Texas	Louisiana
1992	337,934	72,466	288,003	55,917
1993	356,784	75,911	278,841	54,970
1994	377,583	80,871	272,372	56,469
1995	402,097	84,573	245,029	54,824
1996	428,726	87,879	226,052	56,210
1997	468,950	92,286	240,872	61,458
1998	511,964	97,458	238,944	64,473
1999	539,527	99,052	219,844	54,573
2000	586,587	103,630	216,260	55,086
Percentage Change – 3-Year Moving Average 1992-1994=100				
1993-1995	5.98	5.28	-1.60	-0.65
1994-1996	6.33	4.96	-6.63	0.75
1995-1997	7.56	4.51	-4.24	2.98
1996-1998	8.45	4.87	-0.85	5.59
1997-1999	7.86	4.02	-0.88	-0.90
1998-2000	7.74	3.93	-3.52	-3.53
Average	7.32	4.59	-2.95	0.71

Source: U.S. Bureau of Labor Statistics (Website: http//www.bls.gov.).

6.5. Conclusions

The Port of Galveston backed by a much larger industrial base in the Houston area is strategically located to play an important role as a service base for the offshore oil and gas industry. The technological and scientific challenges faced by the industry as it moves to ultra-deep-sea exploration will require more contributions from the Galveston-Houston industrial base. The Port of Galveston is located as an outpost with proximity to many areas that can deliver these services.

Further, the port with its 40 ft access channel and corresponding infrastructure, is strategically located to serve the expanding OCS-deepwater logistical needs. Overall, the OCS service sector at the Port has expanded its capacity during the last decade and is poised to serve the increasing demand for services in the WPA as well as international markets.

REFERENCES

Baud, R.D, R. Peterson, G. E. Richardson, L. S. French, J. Regg, T. Montgomery, T. S. Williams, C. Doyle and M. Dorner. 2002. Deepwater Gulf of Mexico 2002: America's Expanding Frontier. Minerals Management Service, Gulf of Mexico OCS Region, OCS Report, 2002-021. New Orleans, LA. 133 p.

Benefit-Cost Analysis for Acadiana Gulf of Mexico Access Channel (AGMAC). 2001. A Report prepared by Coastal Engineering and Environmental Consultants, Inc. for the Port of Iberia, New Iberia, Louisiana.

Louisiana Department of Transportation and Development. 2001. Port Construction and Development Priority Program, Eighth Annual Report.

Port Fourchon Feasibility Study, August 1994. Environmental Impact Statement, Main Report, U.S. Army Corps of Engineers, New Orleans District.

Port of Iberia. 2000. Master Development Plan. New Iberia, Louisiana.

URS and Greiner-Clyde. 1999. Preliminary Implementation Plan for the OCS Intermodal Support Corridor. Report prepared for the U.S. Army Corps of Engineers, New Orleans District.

U. S. Army Corps of Engineers, Port Fourchon, Feasibility Study. 1994. Main Report, Environmental Impact Statement.

U. S. Army Corps of Engineers. 2001. Waterborne Commerce of the United States, Part 2-Waterways and Harbors, Gulf Coast, Mississippi River System and Antilles. (Website: http://ntl.bts.gov/lib/23000/23500/23560/wcusmvgc01.pdf).

U. S. Bureau of Labor Statistics (Website: http://www.bls.gov).

Appendix A: Data and Regression Model Output - Port Fourchon

Appendix A: Table A.1 1 The Data Used in Regression Models - Port Fourchon

Year	OCS Activities			Miles of Pipe Lines Appd	Southbound Trucks-LA1	Galliano Br Openings	Fuel - Tons Millions	Water - Tons Millions	Dry Cargo Tons Miin.	Cargo Total Tons Miln
	Dev Wells	Expl Wells	OCS total							
	(1)	(2)	(3)	(4)	(5)	(6)	(7)	(8)	(9)	(10)
1992	27	7	34	76						3.900
1993	29	12	41	52		4,188				4.900
1994	37	28	65	193	87,235	4,383				6.800
1995	51	34	85	139	98,550	4,492				7.300
1996	71	42	113	329	116,435	4,599	0 453	2 261	6.278	8.992
1997	88	84	172	285	144,175	4,623	0 219	2 040	8.827	11.086
1998	57	112	169	450	146,365	5,089	0 511	2 511	12.989	16.011
1999	49	123	172	512	151,110	4,643	0 510	3 740	15.521	19.771
2000	67	146	213	241	168,630	5,218	0 693	3 527	20.992	25.212
2001	60	148	208	711	211,335	5,717	0 883	3 856	22.468	27.207

Truck Traffic Relationships

Regression Model 1:1

Independent Variable:	Column (3)	Total Number of OCS Wells Drilled	1994-2001
Dependent Variable:	Column (5)	Southbound Truck Traffic on La 1	1994-2001

SUMMARY OUTPUT

Regression Statistics	
Multiple R	0.933966808
R Square	0.872293999
Adjusted R Square	0.851009666
Standard Error	15402.06323
Observations	8

ANOVA

	df	SS	MS	F	Significance F
Regression	1	9722112312	9722112312	40.982914	0.000684646
Residual	6	1423341310	237223552		
Total	7	11145453622			

	Coefficients	Standard Error	t Stat	P-value	Lower 95%	Upper 95%	Lower 95.0%	Upper 95.0%
Intercept	39816.66793	16640.36812	2.39277567	0.0538222	-900 875811	80534.21167	-900.875811	80534.21167
X Variable 1	672.7666304	105.0903956	6.40178987	0.0006846	415.6195078	929.9137529	415.6195078	929.9137529

Appendix A: Data and Regression Model Output - Port Fourchon (Contd.)

Regression Model 1. 2:

	Independent Variable:	Column (2)	Number of OCS Exploratory Wells Drilled	1994-2001	
	Dependent Variable:	Column (5)	Southbound Truck Traffic on La 1	1994-2001	

SUMMARY OUTPUT

Regression Statistics	
Multiple R	0.929959671
R Square	0.864824989
Adjusted R Square	0.842295821
Standard Error	15846.06584
Observations	8

ANOVA

	df	SS	MS	F	Significance F
Regression	1	9638866807	9638866807	38.386902	0.000814492
Residual	6	1506586815	251097802		
Total	7	11145453622			

	Coefficients	Standard Error	t Stat	P-value	Lower 95%	Upper 95%	Lower 95.0%	Upper 95.0%
Intercept	73757.39041	12139.17948	6.07597824	0.0009028	44053.86655	103460.9143	44053.86655	103460.9143
X Variable 1	744.4572897	120.1567722	6.19571645	0.0008145	450.4440447	1038.470535	450.4440447	1038.470535

Regression Model 1. 3:

	Independent Variable (lag):	Column (4)	Miles of Pipelines Approved	1992-1997	
	Dependent Variable:	Column (5)	Southbound Truck Traffic on La 1	1996-2001	

SUMMARY OUTPUT

Regression Statistics	
Multiple R	0.920290751
R Square	0.846935067
Adjusted R Square	0.821424245
Standard Error	16862.07833
Observations	8

ANOVA

	df	SS	MS	F	Significance F
Regression	1	9439475509	9439475509	33.19905	0.001191612
Residual	6	1705978113	284329686		
Total	7	11145453622			

	Coefficients	Standard Error	t Stat	P-value	Lower 95%	Upper 95%	Lower 95.0%	Upper 95.0%
Intercept	85326.79279	11276.72534	7.56662863	0.0002768	57733.61974	112919.9658	57733.61974	112919.9658
X Variable 1	216.7095568	37.61103064	5.7618617	0.0011916	124.6786129	308.7405007	124.6786129	308.7405007

Barge Traffic Relationships

Regression Model 2. 1:

Independent Variable:	Column (3)	Total Number of OCS Wells Drilled	1993-2001
Dependent Variable:	Column (6)	Galliano Bridge Openings	1993-2001

SUMMARY OUTPUT

Regression Statistics	
Multiple R	0.843739647
R Square	0.711896591
Adjusted R Square	0.670738961
Standard Error	274.5902388
Observations	9

ANOVA

	df	SS	MS	F	Significance F
Regression	1	1304177.628	1304177.63	17.296832	0.004247346
Residual	7	527798.5945	75399.7992		
Total	8	1831976.222			

	Coefficients	Standard Error	t Stat	P-value	Lower 95%	Upper 95%	Lower 95.0%	Upper 95.0%
Intercept	3893 852402	230.2299111	16.9128867	6.188E-07	3349.44556	4438.259244	3349.44556	4438.259244
X Variable 1	6.38717963	1 535768841	4.15894597	0.0042473	2.755665982	10 01869328	2.755665982	10.01869328

Regression Model 2. 2:

Independent Variable:	Column (2)	Number of OCS Exploratory Wells Drilled	1997-2001
Dependent Variable:	Column (6)	Galliano Bridge Openings	1997-2001

SUMMARY OUTPUT

Regression Statistics	
Multiple R	0.867471379
R Square	0.752506593
Adjusted R Square	0.717150392
Standard Error	254.5028871
Observations	9

ANOVA

	df	SS	MS	F	Significance F
Regression	1	1378574.185	1378574.19	21.283582	0.00244509
Residual	7	453402.0368	64771.7195		
Total	8	1831976.222			

	Coefficients	Standard Error	t Stat	P-value	Lower 95%	Upper 95%	Lower 95.0%	Upper 95.0%
Intercept	4141.88145	160.867583	25.7471479	3.408E-08	3761.490334	4522.272566	3761.490334	4522.272566
X Variable 1	7.784728328	1.687411885	4.61341324	0.0024451	3.794636117	11.77482054	3.794636117	11.77482054

Regression Model 2. 3:

Independent Variable (Lag)	Column (4)	Miles of Pipelines Approved	1993-1997
Dependent Variable:	Column (6)	Galliano Bridge Openings	1997-2001

SUMMARY OUTPUT

Regression Statistics	
Multiple R	0 934685194
R Square	0 873636413
Adjusted R Square	0 852575815
Standard Error	174 6124618
Observations	8

ANOVA

	df	SS	MS	F	Significance F
Regression	1	1264766 929	1264766 93	41 482033	0 000662909
Residual	6	182937 071	30489 5118		
Total	7	1447704			

	Coefficients	Standard Error	t Stat	P-value	Lower 95%	Upper 95%	Lower 95.0%	Upper 95.0%
Intercept	4207 093692	116 7742632	36 0275764	3 05E-08	3921 357155	4492 83023	3921 357155	4492 83023
X Variable 1	2 508472721	0 389474804	6 44065469	0 0006629	1 555461511	3 461483932	1 555461511	3 461483932

Cargo Tonnage Relationships

Regression Model 3.1:

Independent Variable:	Column (3)	Total Number of OCS Wells Drilled	1992-2001
Dependent Variable:	Column (10)	Total Port Tonnage	1992-2001

SUMMARY OUTPUT

Regression Statistics	
Multiple R	0.920496089
R Square	0.84731305
Adjusted R Square	0.828227181
Standard Error	3.508133912
Observations	10

ANOVA

	df	SS	MS	F	Significance F
Regression	1	546.3667825	546.366783	44.394785	0.000158666
Residual	8	98.45602838	12.3070035		
Total	9	644.8228109			

	Coefficients	Standard Error	t Stat	P-value	Lower 95%	Upper 95%	Lower 95.0%	Upper 95.0%
Intercept	-1.45615164	2.452572769	0.59372413	0.5690997	-7.11179825	4.199494959	-7.11179825	4.199494959
X Variable 1	0.114575878	0 017195991	6.6629412	0.0001587	0.074921825	0.15422993	0.074921825	0.15422993

Appendix A: Data and Regression Model Output - Port Fourchon (Contd.)

Regression Model 3.2:

Independent Variable	Column (2)	Number of OCS Exploratory Wells Drilled	1992-2001
Dependent Variable:	Column (10)	Total Port Tonnage	1992-2001

SUMMARY OUTPUT

Regression Statistics	
Multiple R	0.973244081
R Square	0.947204041
Adjusted R Square	0.940604546
Standard Error	2.062887509
Observations	10

ANOVA

	df	SS	MS	F	Significance F
Regression	1	610.7787719	610.778772	143.52675	2.17093E-06
Residual	8	34.04403899	4.25550487		
Total	9	644.8228109			

	Coefficients	Standard Error	t Stat	P-value	Lower 95%	Upper 95%	Lower 95.0%	Upper 95.0%
Intercept	2.184254665	1.121810437	1.94708	0.0873855	-0.40264652	4.771155845	-0.40264652	4.771155845
X Variable 1	0.148554964	0 012399973	11.9802649	2.171E-06	0.119960556	0.177149372	0.119960556	0.177149372

Regression Model 3.3:

Independent Variable	Column (2)	Miles of Pipelines Approved	1992-1999
Dependent Variable:	Column (10)	Total Port Tonnage	1994-2001

SUMMARY OUTPUT

Regression Statistics	
Multiple R	0.963279116
R Square	0.927906656
Adjusted R Square	0.915891099
Standard Error	2.336426392
Observations	8

ANOVA

	df	SS	MS	F	Significance F
Regression	1	421.5650302	421.56503	77.225436	0.000120404
Residual	6	32.75332971	5.45888828		
Total	7	454.3183599			

	Coefficients	Standard Error	t Stat	P-value	Lower 95%	Upper 95%	Lower 95.0%	Upper 95.0%
Intercept	3.642054841	1.562514311	2.33089375	0.0585691	-0.18128274	7.465392422	-0.18128274	7.465392422
X Variable 1	0.045796936	0 005211422	8.78780043	0.0001204	0.033045036	0.058548835	0.033045036	0.058548835

85

Appendix A: Table A.1..2 Cargo Handles at Port Fourchon, 1996-2000 Monthly Average (1000 tons)

Month	Gen/bulk	Fuel	Water	Crew Change # people
January	902 5	39.2	168	11.3
February	935 5	27.3	176.2	18.3
March	1088 6	38.5	239.2	11.3
April	1012 9	31.6	223.4	11.5
May	915 1	36	215.5	11.5
June	1030 1	35.9	212.4	11.8
July	1043 7	36.8	240.4	15
August	1063 4	37.6	224.4	13.7
September	1232 6	41	362.1	15
october	1289 9	39	225.8	15
November	1281 3	37	252.4	14.4
December	1072.3	39.2	276.2	14.4
	12867 9	439 1	2816	163 2

Regression Models by Cargo Type

Model 1.4

Independent variable:	Total OCS wells drilled
Dependent variable:	Tonnage water

water/total wells

SUMMARY OUTPUT

Regression Statistics	
Multiple R	0.674078762
R Square	0.454382178
Adjusted R Square	0.317977722
Standard Error	0.667271916
Observations	6

ANOVA

	df	SS	MS	F	Significance F
Regression	1	1.483195593	1.48319559	3.3311388	0.142026544
Residual	4	1.781007241	0.44525181		
Total	5	3.264202833			

	Coefficients	Standard Error	t Stat	P-value	Lower 95%	Upper 95%	Lower 95.0%	Upper 95.0%
Intercept	0.338799492	1.477474455	0.22930988	0.829876	-3.76333572	4.440934707	3.76333572	4.440934707
X Variable 1	0.015188351	0 008321742	1.82514077	0.1420265	-0.00791656	0.038293258	0.00791656	0.038293258

Appendix A: Data and Regression Model Output - Port Fourchon (Contd.)

Model 2:4   Independent variable: Exploratory wells drilled

Dependent variable: Tonnage water

SUMMARY OUTPUT

Regression Statistics	
Multiple R	0.826547799
R Square	0.683181264
Adjusted R Square	0.60397658
Standard Error	0.508468439
Observations	6

ANOVA

	df	SS	MS	F	Significance F
Regression	1	2.230042219	2.23004222	8.6255159	0.042519286
Residual	4	1 034160615	0.25854015		
Total	5	3.264202833			

	Coefficients	Standard Error	t Stat	P-value	Lower 95%	Upper 95%	Lower 95.0%	Upper 95.0%
Intercept	1.189857166	0.646862886	1.83942717	0.1396912	-0.60612585	2 98584018	-0.60612585	2.98584018
X Variable 1	0.016482224	0 005612073	2.93692287	0.0425193	0.000900581	0.032063868	0.000900581	0.032063868

Model 3:4   Independent variable: Pipeline miles approved (Lag)   1994-1999

Dependent variable: Tonnage water   1996-2001

SUMMARY OUTPUT

Regression Statistics	
Multiple R	0.806987756
R Square	0.651229238
Adjusted R Square	0.564036547
Standard Error	0.533492856
Observations	6

ANOVA

	df	SS	MS	F	Significance F
Regression	1	2.125744323	2.12574432	7.4688513	0.052285377
Residual	4	1.138458511	0.28461463		
Total	5	3 264202833			

	Coefficients	Standard Error	t Stat	P-value	Lower 95%	Upper 95%	Lower 95.0%	Upper 95.0%
Intercept	1.551031737	0.569517444	2.72341393	0.0528005	-0.03020546	3.132268931	-0.03020546	3.132268931
X Variable 1	0.004522437	0.0016548	2.73291992	0.0522854	-7.2035E-05	0.009116909	-7.2035E-05	0.009116909

Model 1.5   Independent variable: Total OCS wells drilled   1996-2001

Dependent variable: Tonnage fuel   1996-2001

SUMMARY OUTPUT

Regression Statistics	
Multiple R	0.5890095
R Square	0 346932191
Adjusted R Square	0.183665239
Standard Error	0 203348053
Observations	6

ANOVA

	df	SS	MS	F	Significance F
Regression	1	0.087867111	0.08786711	2.1249382	0.218658927
Residual	4	0.165401722	0.04135043		
Total	5	0.253268833			

	Coefficients	Standard Error	t Stat	P-value	Lower 95%	Upper 95%	Lower 95.0%	Upper 95.0%
Intercept	-0.10025621	0.450253556	0.22266613	0.8347032	-1.35036309	1.149850656	-1.35036309	1.149850656
X Variable 1	0 003696788	0.002536013	1.45771679	0.2186589	-0.00334433	0.010737903	-0.00334433	0.010737903

Model 2.5   Independent variable: Exploratory wells drilled   1996-2001

Dependent variable: Tonnage fuel   1996-2001

SUMMARY OUTPUT

Regression Statistics	
Multiple R	0.710145739
R Square	0 504306971
Adjusted R Square	0 380383714
Standard Error	0.177160658
Observations	6

ANOVA

	df	SS	MS	F	Significance F
Regression	1	0.127725238	0.12772524	4.0695103	0.113847114
Residual	4	0.125543595	0.0313859		
Total	5	0.253268833			

	Coefficients	Standard Error	t Stat	P-value	Lower 95%	Upper 95%	Lower 95.0%	Upper 95.0%
Intercept	0.114219784	0.225380074	0.50678741	0.6389641	-0.51153692	0.739976484	-0.51153692	0.739976484
X Variable 1	0 003944552	0.001955359	2.01730273	0.1138471	-0.00148441	0.009373511	-0.00148441	0.009373511

Model 3.5

Independent variable:	Pipeline miles approved (Lag)	1994-1999
Dependent variable:	Tonnage fuel	1996-2001

SUMMARY OUTPUT

Regression Statistics

Multiple R	0.959919163
R Square	0.9214448
Adjusted R Square	0 901806
Standard Error	0.070525853
Observations	6

ANOVA

	df	SS	MS	F	Significance F
Regression	1	0.233373249	0.23337325	46.919608	0.002377516
Residual	4	0 019895584	0.0049739		
Total	5	0 253268833			

	Coefficients	Standard Error	t Stat	P-value	Lower 95%	Upper 95%	Lower 95.0%	Upper 95.0%
Intercept	0.068325925	0.075288175	0.90752531	0.4154587	-0.14070799	0.277359844	-0.14070799	0.277359844
X Variable 1	0.001498451	0 000218759	6.8497889	0.0023775	0.000891078	0.002105824	0.000891078	0.002105824

Model 1.6

Independent variable:	Total OCS wells drilled	1996-2001
Dependent variable:	General/bulk cargo tonnage	1996-2001

SUMMARY OUTPUT

Regression Statistics	
Multiple R	0.899840082
R Square	0.809712174
Adjusted R Square	0.762140217
Standard Error	3.151246889
Observations	6

ANOVA

	df	SS	MS	F	Significance F
Regression	1	169.0224977	169.022498	17.020788	0.014545611
Residual	4	39.72142782	9.93035696		
Total	5	208.7439255			

	Coefficients	Standard Error	t Stat	P-value	Lower 95%	Upper 95%	Lower 95.0%	Upper 95.0%
Intercept	-13.7805058	6.97749548	1.97499315	0.1194844	-33.1531791	5.592167504	-33.1531791	5.592167504
X Variable 1	0.162137569	0 039300116	4.12562574	0.0145456	0.053022729	0.271252409	0.053022729	0.271252409

89

Model 2.6

Independent variable:	Exploratory wells drilled	1996-2001	
	General/bulk cargo		
Dependent variable:	tonnage	1996-2001	

SUMMARY OUTPUT

Regression Statistics	
Multiple R	0.957509873
R Square	0.916825158
Adjusted R Square	0.896031447
Standard Error	2.083401252
Observations	6

ANOVA

	df	SS	MS	F	Significance F
Regression	1	191.3816824	191.381682	44.091465	0.00266976
Residual	4	17.36224311	4.34056078		
Total	5	208.7439255			

	Coefficients	Standard Error	t Stat	P-value	Lower 95%	Upper 95%	Lower 95.0%	Upper 95.0%
Intercept	-2.15611496	2.650459385	0.81348727	0.461588	-9.51498519	5.202755271	-9.51498519	5.202755271
X Variable 1	0.152689603	0 022994936	6.64014041	0.0026698	0.088845293	0.216533912	0.088845293	0.216533912

Model 3.6

Independent variable:	Pipeline miles approved (Lag)	1994-1999	
Dependent variable:	Tonnage Gen/bulk cargo	1996-2001	

SUMMARY OUTPUT

Regression Statistics	
Multiple R	0.943695959
R Square	0.890562063
Adjusted R Square	0.863202579
Standard Error	2.389796253
Observations	6

ANOVA

	df	SS	MS	F	Significance F
Regression	1	185.899421	185.899421	32.550397	0.004665972
Residual	4	22.84450453	5.71112613		
Total	5	208.7439255			

	Coefficients	Standard Error	t Stat	P-value	Lower 95%	Upper 95%	Lower 95.0%	Upper 95.0%
Intercept	1.063712265	2.551169406	0.41695086	0.6981189	-6.01948421	8.146908745	-6.01948421	8.146908745
X Variable 1	0.042291785	0 007412725	5.70529549	0.004666	0.021710719	0.062872851	0.021710719	0.062872851

Appendix A: Data and Regression Model Output for Port Fourchon (Contd.)

Appendix A: Table A 1 3 Port Fourchon, Correlation Matrix for Various Variables

	Column 1	Column 2	Column 3	Column 4	Column 5	Column 6	Column 7	Column 8	Column 9	Column 10
Column 1	1.0000									
Column 2	0.5522	1.0000								
Column 3	0.7333	0.9718	1.0000							
Column 4	0.4331	0.7982	0.7735	1.0000						
Column 5	0.3460	0.9300	0.9340	0.7983	1.0000					
Column 6	0.3966	0.8675	0.8437	0.7801	0.9138	1.0000				
Column 7	-0.5662	0.7101	0.5890	0.6105	0.7993	0.8829	1.0000			
Column 8	-0.6895	0.8265	0.6741	0.5740	0.7461	0.5973	0.8128	1.0000		
Column 9	-0.4831	0.9575	0.8998	0.4818	0.9014	0.8361	0.8631	0.8910	1.0000	
Column 10	0.4482	0.9732	0.9205	0.7913	0.9326	0.9027	0.8743	0.9136	0.9985	1.0000

Notes:

Column 1	Number of OCS Development wells	Column 6	Number of Galliano bridge openings
Column 2	Number of OCS Exploratory wells	Column 7	Fuel tonnage
Column 3	Total Number of OCS wells	Column 8	Water tonnage
Column 4	Miles of Pipelines Approved	Column 9	General/bulk cargo tonnage
Column 5	Annual truck traffic on LA 1	Column 10	Total port tonnage

A: Table A.1.4. Trend Extrapolation Estimates Through 2010 : Port Fourchon

FORECASTING OF PORT ACTIVITIES

| Year | OCS Activities | | OCS total | Miles of Pipelines | Southbound Trucks LA Hwy 1 | Galliano Bridge Openings | Fuel Million Tons | Water Million Tons | Dry Cargo Million Tons | Total Million Tons |
| | Dev Wells | Expl Wells | | | | | | | | |
	(1)	(2)	(3)	(4)	(5)	(6)	(7)	(8)	(9)	(10)
1992	27	7	34	76						3 900
1993	29	12	41	52		4188				4 900
1994	37	28	65	193	87235	4383				6 800
1995	51	34	85	139	98550	4492				7 300
1996	71	42	113	329	116435	4599	0 453	2 261	6 278	8 992
1997	88	84	172	285	144175	4623	0 219	2 04	8 827	11 086
1998	57	112	169	450	146365	5089	0 511	2 511	12 989	16 011
1999	49	123	172	512	151110	4643	0 51	3 74	15 521	19 771
2000	67	146	213	241	168630	5218	0 693	3 527	20 992	25 212
2001	60	148	208	711	211335	5717	0 883	3 856	22 468	27 207
2002	64	166	230	769	227113	5874	0 985	4 246	25 896	29 904
2003	68	184	252	826	242890	6031	1 087	4 637	29 324	32 601
2004	72	202	274	884	258668	6188	1 189	5 027	32 752	35 298
2005	76	220	296	942	274445	6345	1 291	5 418	36 180	37 996
2006	80	238	318	1000	290223	6501	1 393	5 808	39 608	40 693
2007	84	256	339	1057	306000	6658	1 495	6 199	43 035	43 390
2008	88	273	361	1115	321778	6815	1 597	6 589	46 463	46 087
2009	92	291	383	1173	337555	6972	1 699	6 979	49 891	48 784
2010	96	309	405	1230	353333	7129	1 801	7 370	53 319	51 481

Appendix A: Data and Regression Model Output for Port Fourchon (Contd.)

Appendix A: Table A.1 5. Cargo Forecasts Through 2010 for Water, Fuel, and Dry Cargo- Port Fourchon

Year	Water Total wells Model 4 1	Water Exp wells Model 4 2	Water Pipeline s Model 4 3	Fuel Total wells Model 4 4	Fuel Ex wells Model 4 5	Fuel Pipelines Model 4 6	Dry Cargo Total wells Model 4 7	Dry Cargo Exp wells Model 4 8	Dry Cargo Pipelines Model 4 9
2001	3 856	3 856	3 856	0 883	0 883	0 883	22 468	22 468	22 468
2002	4 189	4 152	4 117	0 964	0 954	0 969	26 021	25 205	24 909
2003	4 522	4 448	4 3509	1 045	1 024	1 056	29 575	27 943	27 670
2004	4 855	4 743	4 5848	1 126	1 095	1 142	33 128	30 680	30 431
2005	5 188	5 039	4 8187	1 207	1 166	1 229	36 681	33 417	33 192
2006	5 520	5 335	5 0526	1 288	1 236	1 315	40 235	36 155	35 953
2007	5 853	5 631	5 2865	1 369	1 307	1 402	43 788	38 892	38 714
2008	6 186	5 927	5 5204	1 450	1 377	1 488	47 341	41 629	41 475
2009	6 519	6 222	5 7543	1 531	1 448	1 575	50 895	44 367	44 236
2010	6 852	6 518	5 9882	1 612	1 519	1 661	54 448	47 104	46 997

Appendix B: Data and Regression Model Output - Port of Morgan City

Appendix B: Table 1 The Data and Variables Used In the Analysis

	Dev. Wells	Expl. Wells	Total Wells	Pipeliine miles	EP	DOCD	Self-prop Vessel Trips	Non SP Vessel Trips	Total Vessel trips
1992	27	7	34	76	25	3	18398	2112	20510
1993	29	12	41	52	25	4	21540	2225	23765
1994	37	28	65	193	37	4	23421	2515	25936
1995	51	34	85	139	38	8	25302	2805	28107
1996	71	42	113	329	64	10	28367	3643	32010
1997	88	84	172	285	105	11	30168	4371	34539
1998	57	112	169	450	125	16	22983	4095	27078
1999	49	123	172	512	168	14	15479	3127	18606
2000	67	146	213	241	157	27	18753	4266	23019
2001	60	148	208	711	150	37	--	--	---

Appendix B: Table 2 Correlation Matrix Indicating Variable Relationships for Morgan City

	Column 1	Column 2	Column 3	Column 4	Column 5	Column 6	Column 7	Column 8	Column 9
Column 1	1								
Column 2	0.5675412	1							
Column 3	0.758536	0.9670177	1						
Column 4	0.4932071	0.7422342	0.7400146	1					
Column 5	0.5407655	0.9810721	0.943754	0.8058073	1				
Column 6	0.5744607	0.9250053	0.9098042	0.5271029	0.8614299	1			
Column 7	0.5946418	-0.2571051	-0.0195263	-0.0730038	-0.3066105	-0.2043403	1		
Column 8	0.9149284	0.786163	0.9052451	0.6154918	0.7331255	0.7901586	0.3582037	1	
Column 9	0.7071948	-0.1033986	0.136943	0.0378146	-0.1583129	-0.053865	0.9871359	0.5028699	1

Column (1)	Number of Development wells drilled
Column 2	Number of Exploratory Wells drilled
Column 3	Total Number of wells drilled
Column 4	Miles of Pipeline Approvals
Column 5	Number of Exploration Plans Filed
Column 6	Number of DOCDs Filed
Column 7	Number of Self-Propelled Vessel trips
Column 8	Number of None Self-Propelled Vessel trips
Column 9	Number of Total Vessel trips

Regression Model 4:1

	Dependent Variable:	Column (8): Number of non self-propelled vessel trips 1992-2000
	Independent Variable:	Column (1) Number of Development wells drilled 1992-2000

SUMMARY OUTPUT

Regression Statistics

Multiple R	0.9149284
R Square	0.837094
Adjusted R Square	0.8138217
Standard Error	381.54916
Observations	9

ANOVA

	df	SS	MS	F	Significance F
Regression	1	5236440.5	5236440.5	35.969564	0.0005436
Residual	7	1019058.3	145579.76		
Total	8	6255498.9			

	Coefficients	Standard Error	t Stat	P-value	Lower 95%	Upper 95%	Lower 95.0%	Upper 95.0%
Intercept	1129.5222	374.15591	3.0188542	0.0194177	244.78465	2014.2597	244.78465	2014.2597
X Variable 1	39.901892	6.6531284	5.9974631	0.0005436	24.169754	55.634029	24.169754	55.634029

Regression Model 4:2

	Dependent Variable:	Column (8): Number of non self-propelled vessel trips 1992-2000
	Independent Variable:	Column (2) Number of Exploratory Wells drilled 1992-2000

SUMMARY OUTPUT

Regression Statistics

Multiple R	0.786163
R Square	0.6180523
Adjusted R Square	0.5634883
Standard Error	584.2301
Observations	9

ANOVA

	df	SS	MS	F	Significance F
Regression	1	3866225.2	3866225.2	11.327115	0.0119925
Residual	7	2389273.6	341324.81		
Total	8	6255498.9			

	Coefficients	Standard Error	t Stat	P-value	Lower 95%	Upper 95%	Lower 95.0%	Upper 95.0%
Intercept	2364.3071	324.97251	7.2754065	0.0001662	1595.8698	3132.7444	1595.8698	3132.7444
X Variable 1	13.401762	3.9820092	3.3655779	0.0119925	3.9858134	22.817711	3.9858134	22.817711

96

Regression Model 4:3

Dependent Variable:	Column (8):	Number of non self-propelled vessel trips 1992-2000		
Independent Variable:	Column (3)	Total Number of wells drilled		1992-2000

SUMMARY OUTPUT

Regression Statistics

Multiple R	0.9052451
R Square	0.8194688
Adjusted R Square	0.7936786
Standard Error	401.6596
Observations	9

ANOVA

	df	SS	MS	F	Significance F
Regression	1	5126185.9	5126185.9	31.774451	0.0007851
Residual	7	1129313	161330.43		
Total	8	6255498.9			

	Coefficients	Standard Error	t Stat	P-value	Lower 95%	Upper 95%	Lower 95.0%	Upper 95.0%
Intercept	1795.9972	289.03078	6.2138614	0.0004393	1112.5485	2479.4459	1112.5485	2479.4459
X Variable 1	12.213369	2.1666884	5.6368831	0.0007851	7.089969	17.33677	7.089969	17.33677

Regression Model 4:4

Dependent Variable:	Column (8):	Number of non self-propelled vessel trips 1993-2000		
Independent Variable: (Lag)	Column (4)	Miles of Pipeline Approvals		1992-1999

SUMMARY OUTPUT

Regression Statistics	
Multiple R	0.6708839
R Square	0.4500852
Adjusted R Square	0.3584327
Standard Error	664.95377
Observations	8

ANOVA

	df	SS	MS	F	Significance F
Regression	1	2171367.8	2171367.8	4.9107802	0.0685718
Residual	6	2652981.1	442163.51		
Total	7	4824348.9			

	Coefficients	Standard Error	t Stat	P-value	Lower 95%	Upper 95%	Lower 95.0%	Upper 95.0%
Intercept	2544.3891	444.69613	5.7216354	0.0012357	1456.2561	3632.5221	1456.2561	3632.5221
X Variable 1	3.2867815	1.4831859	2.216028	0.0685718	-0.3424463	6.9160092	0.3424463	6.9160092

Regression Model 4:5

| | Dependent Variable: | Column (8): Number of non self-propelled vessel trips 1992-2000 |
| | Independent Variable: | Column (5) Number of Exploration Plans Filed 1992-2000 |

SUMMARY OUTPUT

Regression Statistics

Multiple R	0.7331255
R Square	0.537473
Adjusted R Square	0.4713977
Standard Error	642.91047
Observations	9

ANOVA

	df	SS	MS	F	Significance F
Regression	1	3362161.8	3362161.8	8.1342518	0.0246157
Residual	7	2893337.1	413333.87		
Total	8	6255498.9			

	Coefficients	Standard Error	t Stat	P-value	Lower 95%	Upper 95%	Lower 95.0%	Upper 95.0%
Intercept	2303.0358	392.20781	5.8719784	0.0006167	1375.6124	3230.4592	1375.6124	3230.4592
X Variable 1	11.3329	3.9735828	2.852061	0.0246157	1.9368769	20.728924	1.9368769	20.728924

Regression Model 4:6

| | Dependent Variable: | Column (8): Number of non self-propelled vessel trips 1992-2000 |
| | Independent Variable: | Column (6) Number of DOCDs Filed 1992-2000 |

SUMMARY OUTPUT

Regression Statistics

Multiple R	0.7901586
R Square	0.6243507
Adjusted R Square	0.5706865
Standard Error	579.39302
Observations	9

ANOVA

	df	SS	MS	F	Significance F
Regression	1	3905625	3905625	11.634401	0.0112737
Residual	7	2349873.9	335696.28		
Total	8	6255498.9			

	Coefficients	Standard Error	t Stat	P-value	Lower 95%	Upper 95%	Lower 95.0%	Upper 95.0%
Intercept	2248.4579	348.97687	6.4429997	0.0003526	1423.2593	3073.6565	1423.2593	3073.6565
X Variable 1	91.988445	26.968778	3.4109237	0.0112737	28.217464	155.75943	28.217464	155.75943

The Department of the Interior Mission

As the Nation's principal conservation agency, the Department of the Interior has responsibility for most of our nationally owned public lands and natural resources. This includes fostering sound use of our land and water resources; protecting our fish, wildlife, and biological diversity; preserving the environmental and cultural values of our national parks and historical places; and providing for the enjoyment of life through outdoor recreation. The Department assesses our energy and mineral resources and works to ensure that their development is in the best interests of all our people by encouraging stewardship and citizen participation in their care. The Department also has a major responsibility for American Indian reservation communities and for people who live in island territories under U.S. administration.

The Minerals Management Service Mission

As a bureau of the Department of the Interior, the Minerals Management Service's (MMS) primary responsibilities are to manage the mineral resources located on the Nation's Outer Continental Shelf (OCS), collect revenue from the Federal OCS and onshore Federal and Indian lands, and distribute those revenues.

Moreover, in working to meet its responsibilities, the **Offshore Minerals Management Program** administers the OCS competitive leasing program and oversees the safe and environmentally sound exploration and production of our Nation's offshore natural gas, oil and other mineral resources. The MMS **Minerals Revenue Management** meets its responsibilities by ensuring the efficient, timely and accurate collection and disbursement of revenue from mineral leasing and production due to Indian tribes and allottees, States and the U.S. Treasury.

The MMS strives to fulfill its responsibilities through the general guiding principles of: (1) being responsive to the public's concerns and interests by maintaining a dialogue with all potentially affected parties and (2) carrying out its programs with an emphasis on working to enhance the quality of life for all Americans by lending MMS assistance and expertise to economic development and environmental protection.

www.ingramcontent.com/pod-product-compliance
Lightning Source LLC
Chambersburg PA
CBHW052001280526
45793CB00005B/813